TRANSFORMED BY HIS GLORY

Transformed
by His
GLORY

Revealing God
Through the
Fruit of the Spirit

ALETHA HINTHORN

Beacon Hill Press of Kansas City
Kansas City, Missouri

ISBN 083-411-7789

Printed in the
United States of America

Cover Design: Kevin Williamson

Library of Congress Cataloging-in-Publication Data

Hinthorn, Aletha.
    Transformed by his glory : revealing God through the fruit of the Spirit / Aletha Hinthorn.
        p. cm.
    Includes bibliographical references.
    ISBN 0-8341-1778-9 (pbk.)
    1. Fruit of the Spirit. 2. Christian life. I. Title
BV4501.2 .H5226 2000
234'.13—dc21

                                                                    00-022515

10   9   8   7   6   5   4   3   2   1

CONTENTS

Preface   7

Introduction   9

  1. Christ in Us, the Hope of Glory   13

  2. Love   23

  3. Joy   33

  4. Peace   43

  5. Patience   55

  6. Kindness   65

  7. Goodness   77

  8. Faithfulness   87

  9. Meekness (Gentleness)   99

10. Self-Control   109

Leaders' Guide   121

Notes   131

PREFACE

ONE DAY when my children were small, I knelt down in our upstairs bedroom and prayed, *Dear Lord, let me work for You full time.* Months later I wrote a response to that prayer in my journal: "God has answered my prayer—yet I'm not teaching Bible studies or writing every day. Some days I'm doing homework with Gregg, taking Arla to the park, having lunch with Daniel, or visiting with a friend. I've learned that working for God means establishing scriptural priorities and living by them."

Perhaps I prayed that prayer because earlier I had come across Hannah's words of worship after she had taken Samuel to the temple: "There is no one besides you" (1 Sam. 2:2). I recall sitting at the kitchen table and saying aloud, "Hannah, you know something I don't." I really didn't think I could say, *There's no one but You, God.* Yes, God was big in my life, but there were my family, friends, and all the activities I was involved in.

Hannah's words and attitude challenged me. I titled a page in my notebook "One Goal" and began collecting names of those who appeared to have one goal for all of their lives. I noticed that David said, "One thing have I desired of the LORD, that will I seek after; that I may dwell in the house of the LORD all the days of my life" (Ps. 27:4, KJV). Paul said, "This one thing I do" (Phil. 3:13, KJV). Jesus told Martha that she was troubled about many things but "only one thing is needed" (Luke 10:42).

Then I found Paul's words to the Corinthians, "Whatever you do, do it all for the glory of God" (1 Cor. 10:31). I learned that to do all for the glory of God meant that at any moment I could lift whatever I was doing and say, "I'm doing this for You, Lord."

It also meant that all my attitudes were to be determined by what would please Him. Paul's declaration "I re-
solved to know nothing while I was with you except Jesus
Christ" (1 Cor. 2:2) became very practical. My focus was to
be on Jesus. What was He thinking about my actions and
attitudes? I would resolve to care only that I had His approval!

When we're consumed with a passion to do all for the
glory of God, when we're filled with that one desire to
please Him and to have His presence be at home within
us, what will be the result? Others will see the glory of His
presence in our lives!

Two thousand years ago Christ came into human form and showed the world God's glory. "The Word became flesh and made his dwelling among us" (John 1:14). As we apply scripture to our lives, the Word again becomes flesh. Our part is to continually surrender to the Spirit of Christ so that each moment He is welcomed to live His life through us.
As we do, once again others will behold His glory.

INTRODUCTION

IN THE FALL OF 1998, Nazarene Theological Seminary in Kansas City honored Dennis Kinlaw as "Preacher of the Year" and invited him to give a week of sermons. One of those messages dealt with levels of intimacy with God. Dr. Kinlaw described the most intimate level as that of *identification*.

What does it mean to identify with God? Paul explained it when he said, "I have been crucified with Christ and I no longer live, but Christ lives in me" (Gal. 2:20).

This means we're dead to our selfish desires, but what else? "This means they see not me, but Christ," Dr. Kinlaw said. We're to be Christ to others.

With this concept in my mind, I thought of the young woman who was to visit me that afternoon of the day I heard this sermon. As I prayed for her, I asked the Lord to allow me to be Christ to her. I did not know her needs, but I would rest in the Holy Spirit and trust Him to express himself through me.

During our visit, I looked to the Lord moment by moment to give me what she needed. The next day, I received a bouquet of flowers and this note: "Thanks for the peace you brought me through Christ."

When we're with others, we bring to them the presence of Christ. We may be unsure what to say or do, but as we depend upon Him, He enables us to express His love.

Just like Jesus

Through Jesus we learn how to allow God to express Himself through us. In John 8:28 Jesus declared, "I do nothing on my own but speak just what the Father has taught me." When He said, "The Father who sent me commanded me what to say and how to say it. . . . Whatever I say is just what the Father has told me to say" (John 12:49-50), it seems as though He's saying His Father gave Him both the content and the exact words!

Jesus' life is the pattern for our life. He never tried to be independent but continually received His spiritual life from the Father. He wants that same dependence to be in us. "I live by the power of the living Father who sent me; in the same way, those who partake of me will live because of me" (John 6:57, NLT).

John 14 gives a striking statement of the possibility of our being as dependent upon the Father for everything as Jesus was. Jesus told the disciples that they had seen the Father when they saw Him. Philip didn't understand the truth that to see Him—to see Jesus' spirit—was the same as seeing the Father.

Disappointed, Jesus asked, "Don't you know me, Philip?" (v. 9). He was not saying to Philip, "See My physical body," but "Philip, if you see My gentle and loving spirit, you've seen God. He and I have the same spirit."

The wording of the next verse makes me think that perhaps He leaned toward them, lowering His voice as though His words would be breathtaking. Indeed they were.

"I assure you, most solemnly I tell you, if anyone steadfastly believes in Me, he will himself be able to do the things that I do" (John 14:12, AMP.).

We should be able to say to others, as Jesus said to Philip, "If you see Me, you've seen God. The words I say to you are not My own." When united with the Spirit of God, our spirit will be the same as the spirit of Jesus.

The Goal of This Book

God is Spirit, and He'll reveal himself through our spirits. That's why this book is on the fruit of the Spirit. If we're going to show Christ to the world, it will be through His love, joy, and peace, which enables us to be consistently kind, patient, and good. His faithfulness, gentleness, and self-control will characterize our lives.

Others may not understand that they're seeing Christ, just as Philip did not realize He had seen God, but the impact of His Spirit will be made.

Paul spoke of the *fruit* of the Spirit—not *fruits*—because it's one fruit. If our attitude is truly an expression of the Holy Spirit, then all aspects of the fruit will be present. The Holy Spirit will not produce a rigid, unkind self-control, a superficial goodness, or a faithfulness that is more legalistic than loving.

The Holy Spirit comes to indwell us as a Friend and Helper, a Teacher and a Guide—but not as a puppeteer. Being controlled by Him does not mean He acts through us against our wishes. We live by the Holy Spirit's promptings and power, thinking and choosing with His aid. Our faith and obedience allow Him to reveal himself through us.

We trust the Holy Spirit to express His love through our personalities, and He delights in doing so. He likes the personality He created in each of us. We're never more ourselves than when Christ lives through us.

To produce the fruit of the Spirit, we must depend upon Christ within us, just as He depended on the Father. In the following chapters we will consider what life is like when the Holy Spirit is bearing fruit within us. It's a cooperative effort. Our efforts to be loving, joyful, patient, and faithful represent our faith and obedience. Our faith and obedience are the setting of our sails so we can receive with the empowering of the Holy Spirit. Then we can be Christ to others.

Chapter 1 focuses on how to have the "mind . . .

which was . . . in Christ Jesus" (Phil. 2:5, KJV). Each of the remaining nine chapters examines a fruit of the Holy Spirit.

"For to me, to live is Christ" (Phil. 1:21). "Paul might have been saying two things with that statement," explains Dennis Kinlaw. "First, 'for . . . me, to live is Christ' because He's the source of my life.' Second, 'for . . . me to live is Christ' because I represent Christ to other people.' To paraphrase that thought, 'For me to live is for you to know Christ.'"[1]

The goal of this study is for us to be able to say: "For me to live is for my family, friends, and coworkers to see the glory of Christ's presence in my life." May the Holy Spirit make this statement a reality in our lives.

1

CHRIST IN US, THE HOPE OF GLORY

I used to ask God to help me. Then I asked God if I might help Him.
I ended up by asking Him to do His work through me.
—Hudson Taylor

JANET, MY NEXT-DOOR NEIGHBOR, came to Christ after we began a neighborhood Bible study. She fell in love with the Word, memorizing it and often quoting it in prayer. Her desire to live by the Word and to please the Lord became almost palpable.

One day she shared an encounter she and her husband, Sid, had on their way to Colorado. Before leaving, Janet and Sid asked the Lord to use them on the highway. About three hours down the road they stopped for breakfast and again prayed, *Lord, use us on the highway.*

"We meant it sincerely," she said.

Within three miles the traffic came to a stop. Janet looked ahead and saw that there had been an accident. *Lord, what now—what do You want us to do?* she prayed. Immediately she knew God wanted her to go to the scene of the accident. *Lord, I've just had breakfast. I don't know if I can handle this,* she told Him. But she opened the door, and she and Sid walked past the 10 vehicles between their car and the overturned one.

"Is there anyone in the car?" Janet asked the other travelers standing around.

"One lady, and she's pinned in." Janet walked closer and could see the woman's hand. A truck driver who had stopped to help was trying to hold the passenger's head up as she hung upside down.

Janet continued, "Prov. 28:1 says, 'The righteous are as bold as a lion,' and that was one time I was. I went to the truck driver and said, 'I'm a Christian. Would you mind if I pray for this woman?'"

He said that would be fine, so Janet looked at the ground preparing to get down so she could reach the lady's hand. The ground surrounding the lady was covered in oil, and to reach the injured lady's hand, Janet would have to lie in it. She didn't hesitate.

Janet said, "I lay down, took the woman's hand, and saw she was in a terrible shape. Her ribs were broken, and there was broken glass all around her. I began to pray, and every time I said the name 'Jesus,' she squeezed my hand. Soon the truck driver was crying. After praying awhile, I sensed I should quit praying and comfort her. 'Jesus is going to take care of you,' I assured her. After about 15 minutes, the rescue squad came. I got up out of the oil, and Sid and I walked back to our car.

"Later I asked, *Lord, did You really have me do that, or was I doing that in my flesh?*

"He said, 'That wasn't you lying in the oil—that was Me.'"

Longing to please her Lord, Janet had simply followed through on the ideas in her mind and the prompting in her spirit. She found an intimacy with Jesus that made His Spirit at home within her.

"Let This Mind Be in You"

Paul wrote, "Clothe yourselves with the Lord Jesus Christ" (Rom. 13:14). The implication is that we can be so covered with Christ that others see Him and not us. To do this, we must think as Jesus thought. Let's examine a few of His statements that give insight into His way of thinking.

Whatever I say is just what the Father has told me to say (John 12:50).

1. Jesus said He always obeyed the Father's promptings. If He needed to listen attentively, then certainly we do too. Notice in John 8:28-29 and 12:49-50 what Jesus said about His words. *What did He say?*

2. I think Jesus would have had some pretty good things to say on His own! Why do you think Jesus refused to say anything except what the Father gave Him to say?

3. What does John 14:26 say about His willingness to guide our steps and the possibility of our recognizing His guidance?

Trust Him to give you His ideas. It would be very strange if Jesus promised to give us a Counselor who would be with us to teach us at all times but then didn't give us the capacity to hear Him. Be as confident that He will give you His thoughts as you are that air will be there for you to breathe.

4. Learning to respond to the Holy Spirit is actually submitting our minds to the Word. What is one of the functions of the Holy Spirit? Reread John 14:26.

5. We can learn to practice consciously "walking in the Spirit." Too often, though, we tend to respond impulsively like Peter, who drew His sword and chopped off the servant's ear. Then the Lord has to go along behind us, patching things up. To live a surrendered life is to surrender every moment to the deeply interior voice of the Spirit.

Can you think of a time when you acted without the approval of the Spirit's prompting within you? What was the fruit of such action?

6. Let's try to cultivate the pattern of looking to Christ: What is He doing in this situation? How is He responding? *Lord, what is Your will?* or *Lord, give me the mind of Christ.*

Cultivate the habit of recognizing that Christ dwells in your spirit. Many times we have no conscious sense of His presence, but we are to trust that the Spirit indwells us. We do not begin with feeling; we begin with acting as though He were with us. Treat Him as if He were in you, and you in Him; and He will respond to your trust. The consciousness of His presence will become real and delightful.

"Can one reach God by toil?" wrote W. B. Yeats. "He gives himself to the pure in heart. He asks nothing but our attention."[2]

Think of a time when you failed to respond as Christ would have. Which of the following aspects of walking in the Spirit were lacking?

___ Willingness to say His words rather than my own
___ Humble dependence upon God
___ Faith that He will give me the mind of Christ

I live because of the Father (John 6:57).

When Jesus said, "I live because of the Father" (John 6:57), He was saying He receives His life continually from the Father. This is an important concept, because He asks that we recognize that we too draw life from Him moment by moment.

1. Consider the significance of the present-tense verbs in John 4:14; 6:56-58.

Dennis Kinlaw wrote, "If the eternal Son cannot do the work of God except in intimate relationship to and dependence upon the Father, it is certain that our own significant fruit will come as we walk with and lean upon the Spirit of the same God."[3]

2. How does John 6:63 sum up the importance of the role of the Spirit?

start here
read again

3. What picture did Jesus use to teach the possibility of our continually receiving the Spirit? See John 15:1-8.

4. List at least two ways in which our life in Christ will be like the vine and branch.

5. For us to remain in Christ is for us to receive His life as continuously as a branch draws sap from the vine. Just as Christ continually draws life from the Father, so we continually draw life from Christ. As long as the branches stay connected to the vine, the sap constantly flows into

these branches. Andrew Murray taught that the sap represents the Holy Spirit.

It is as we continue to draw life from Him that we live.
As we go through our day, we simply look to Christ, asking
Him to give us His thoughts. What is necessary to be fruit-
bearing, according to John 15:6?

When Jesus says, "Remain in me, and I will remain in
you" (John 15:4), He is saying that to the degree that you
remain in Him, He will remain in you. Our constant abiding depends upon our constant fellowship with Him.

The fruitfulness of the branch does not depend upon
itself, but upon Christ, in whom it lives. He will do His part
if the union is maintained.

I always do what pleases him (John 8:29).

Jesus believed that each moment He could be pleasing
the Father. He wants us to have that same confidence.
Donald Grey Barnhouse in his sermon "The Day-by-Day
Christian Life"[4] described his daily activities, showing the
possibility of looking to the Lord for guidance. For instance,
his secretary brings in his mail. "A swift prayer must be
sent heavenward. . . . Every detail has to be done in the
strength of the Lord, in a moment-by-moment looking to
Him. . . . I have come to the place where I never take one
of the letters that are brought to me without a quick prayer
to God for the ability to meet the need."

1. Think of your daily activities. For how many of them
do you consciously depend upon Christ for His strength?

An older godly gentleman told me, "I think most of the time I have the sense of the Holy Spirit's leading. Of course, I tend to pray about most everything."

2. Notice that in 2 Chron. 20 that it was after Jehoshaphat prayed, "Our eyes are upon you" (v. 12), that he received the word "The battle is not yours, but God's" (v. 15).

What do you think Jehoshaphat meant by the phrase "Our eyes are upon you"?

3. It's always that way—as long as our eyes are on the Lord, it's not our battle. We have to remind ourselves of that again and again when we begin to think we have a battle to fight. Can you think of an area in your life in which you're trying to fight a battle yourself?

4. We frequently don't think to ask for specific needs. I had wanted to wake up during the night for devotions, so I asked the Lord to awaken me. He did, and I lay there for a few moments and soon was back to sleep. One night I thought of also asking that He help me *stay* awake. He did!

The Holy Spirit guides continually, and He has promised power for every need—daily work, habits, attitudes. List three areas in which you have never thought of looking to the Holy Spirit to be your strength. Claim the promise of Phil. 4:19.

5. We must keep our eyes on Him. When we're confronted with a need, it just takes a moment to say, *My eyes are on You, Lord.* By this you can mean, *I trust You to give me all I need. I will say and do only what You give me. I trust that the ideas that come to me are Your choice of words, attitudes, actions—not my own. I rest from my own works of trying to manipulate, to control, to strategize.*

Why is having our eyes on the Lord a prerequisite to hearing "The battle is not yours"?

6. If by faith you could say, *My eyes are on You, God. I'm trusting You to fight this battle,* what changes might you—or others—notice in your attitude or actions?

I seek not to please myself (John 5:30).

1. Walking in the Spirit implies that our obedience is so prompt that we're never a step behind Him. Underlying Jesus' prompt obedience to His Father was His desire to please Him. His joy was in doing His Father's wishes. Nothing else mattered to Him. Read John 5:30 and 8:29.

2. The same will be true of all who live as He lived. "Those who live in accordance with the Spirit have their minds set on what the Spirit desires" (Rom. 8:5). What does it mean to have our minds set on something?

3. God wants a relationship with us that is so full of love that everything we do flows out of our desire to please Him. How will this mind-set be evident in our lives?

To love God with all our heart means that we don't find joy in anything unless we know it pleases the One we love.

4. A. W. Tozer encourages us to "keep reminding God in our times of private prayer that we mean every act for His glory; then supplement those times by a thousand thought-prayers as we go about the job of living. Let us practice the fine art of making every work a priestly minis- tration. Let us believe that God is in all our simple deeds and learn to find Him there."[5]

Why is it vital to our living in the Spirit to think often about Him through the day?

5. What is the secret of those who have a loving rela- tionship with God? They've learned to make time for God. Often work crowds our time for worship, but for them, fel- lowship with God crowds their work. While alone with Him, they learn to recognize the voice of the Spirit. A cou- ple who has been married many years often need no more than a silent glance to understand what the other is think- ing. Gaining a sensitivity to the Spirit will come as we spend much time in His presence.

Jesus spent much time alone in prayer. See Mark 1:45 and Luke 5:16. How important to your relationship to God do you consider your time alone with God to be?

6. If our highest joy is in pleasing Him, then our deepest grief will be when we realize that we have grieved the Holy Spirit. When we grieve Him, others are unaware of His presence in us because we're not bearing His fruit.

Instant forgiveness is possible, though. Donald Grey Barnhouse spoke of a phone call alerting him to a newspaper report that bitterly attacked him. "I had not asked the Lord to give me the [help of the] Holy Spirit [in] answering the telephone when it comes rudely into my work." So Dr. Barnhouse answered, "These men are cowards, and they are doing the work of the devil, the accuser of the brethren!"

When Barnhouse hung up, he was restless. He went back to his work, but something was wrong.

Lord, have I offended Thee? he prayed. He quickly asked that His fellowship with the Spirit be restored, and the cloud was gone.[6]

Are you quick to ask forgiveness when you sense you have grieved the Holy Spirit?

Memorize: "Since we live by the Spirit, let us keep in step with the Spirit" (Gal. 5:25).

Prayer: *Dear Lord, You who provided the Israelites with the cloud by day and fire by night and the silver trumpets to alert the whole company when it was time to move, show me the way to go. You are not less concerned about my path. Teach me to heed every impulse of the Holy Spirit, my constant Companion. Guide me to know and obey Your voice, confident that all will be well when I follow You. In Jesus' name I pray. Amen.*

2

LOVE

AGAPĒ, the Greek word for the type of love that's part of the fruit of the Spirit, goes beyond a mere feeling—it is a strong inner commitment that results in a desire to please the one we love. "If you love me, you will obey what I command," Jesus said in John 14:15.

The very essence of God is love. The Bible does not say God is faith, power, or wisdom. God *has* these attributes, but God *is* love (see 1 John 4:16). If we could extract love from God, we would extract His very life.

Paul wrote that without love "I am nothing" (1 Cor. 13:2). If we omit love from our life, actions, and relationships, there's nothing of value left. Pouring love into relationships brings life.

A Portrait of Jesus' Love

When Jesus sat at the Last Supper and announced that one of the disciples would betray Him, no one had a clue that it was Judas. Jesus' loving expression was the same to each of them.

"While we were still sinners, Christ died for us," we read in Rom. 5:8. He loves us enough to express His love to us, even to die for us, before we change.

"Love each other as I have loved you," He says, and He commands us to do only what He enables us to do. With Christ in us, we can love others just as they are.

His Love in Us

Expressing love is a matter of being sensitive to God's Spirit. "A wise man's heart guides his mouth," says Prov.

16:23. When we're listeners to the Holy Spirit, our hearts will teach us how and when to speak and act out of love.

I had accompanied my husband on an out-of-town business trip. As I sat next to a stranger at lunch, I wondered how I was going to make conversation. I thought of Christ's love for her and decided to use our time together to help her sense His love. As I focused on loving her with the love of Christ, conversation came easily. Within minutes she was sharing her difficulties in finding friends in her new neighborhood, her unhappiness with her job. We parted that day as friends.

In 1 Pet. 4:8, Peter wrote, "Above all, love"—perhaps because it's the surest means of doing what the Holy Spirit would do. God is love. God wants to express himself to others through our love, but usually we think He wants to reveal himself through our wisdom.

When in doubt as to what the Holy Spirit desires, we will likely do the right thing if we do the loving thing. One Sunday I was asked to teach a primary Sunday School class. Knowing my lack of skills in this area, I prayed that the Lord would simply help me to show the children His love. We went through the songs and stories while I focused on communicating love. Class was dismissed, we went to the worship service, and I wondered if love had made any difference. To my amazement, immediately after the worship service about half the class came to where I was sitting and looked up to me as if to say, "Love me some more, teacher."

As we trust Christ to relive His own life in us, He will teach us, step-by-step, moment-by-moment, to avoid the things that fall short of love. The Holy Spirit pours out His love into our hearts, causing us to be Christ to others as we respond to His command to love one another. Doing what love would do welcomes the Holy Spirit.

Reflections on His Love

Jude 21 does not say "Keep loving God" but "Keep yourself in God's love." This means we're to keep a constant consciousness and recognition of God's love for us. It's the same thought Jesus expressed in John 15:9-10.

1. Write at least one thought you have as you meditate on these verses.

2. The last phrase of John 15:10 invites us: "Abide in My love" (NASB). We're to do as Frank Laubach said—to stay wrapped in God, which means we stay wrapped in love. When we live in God, we live in an ambiance of love.

No wonder John called himself "the disciple whom Jesus loved" (John 13:23). He lived wrapped in love, so the first thing he thought of regarding Jesus was "He loves me!"

Andrew Murray wrote, "The heavenly Father, who offers to meet us in the inner chamber, has no other object than to fill our hearts with His love."[1] When you're alone with the Lord, allow yourself to receive His love.

Write at least three sentences here or in your prayer journal that you think God would say in reply if you asked, *God, do You love me?*

3. Jesus was never focused on how much He loved himself. He said, "While you are yet sinners, I'll lay down My life for you." Paul put it strongly: "God demonstrates his own love for us in this: While we were still sinners, Christ died for us" (Rom. 5:8).

The Lord gave the command that they should love one

another as He had loved them. Fortunately, we're not left to draw upon our own supply of love, which is little better than a cistern, exhaustible and leaky at best. According to Rom. 5:5 and 1 John 4:7, from where do we get love?

4. God wants our love to increase till it overflows, just as His does for us. See 1 Thess. 3:12. The Greek word for "overflow" means "to superabound, to have enough and to spare, to have an excess." What will be evidences that our love is overflowing for others?

"When I began my new job, there was a coworker who was particularly difficult to work with," John shared in Sunday School. "But I thought as a Christian I should tolerate him. I felt I was doing quite a good job of tolerating him.

"Then I realized God hadn't called me to tolerate people. He called me to *love* them, so I began praying for this man. Soon I realized that I really did love him. Now he's one of my closest coworkers."

We're most like Christ and most used of Him when we're loving others. As we're sensitive to ways to express God's love, all we do will be used of Him.

5. What is Jesus' love causing Him to do even now? See Heb. 7:25.

6. Our love expressed through our intercession is perhaps the most like Christ's love. Let's go to prayer realizing that the Holy Spirit within us loves others passionately; He desires to do them good. As we look to Him, He will share His burden and compassion with us. Consider why intercession is one of the purest expressions of love.

7. One day George Watson felt led to pray for a man who had done much harm to him and his family. At the beginning of his prayer, he tried to feel love for the man by putting himself in the man's place and looking at himself from the man's viewpoint. But the Holy Spirit soon showed him that this was the (human way,) not the divine. He was to love that man with the identical love Jesus had for him— to pity, sympathize with, and feel toward him as God felt by allowing himself to be a channel for God's tender compassion.[2]

He followed the suggestion of the Spirit, and soon he felt a sincere love for him. All the man's concerns became very precious to Mr. Watson. From that time, he found it easy to pray for him and to think of him with a special love.

Why can we not pray in the Spirit unless we love with His love?

8. Wesley Duewel wrote in *Mighty Prevailing Prayer,* "How can Christians be carefree in a hurting world and think they have the heart of Christ? How can Christians be tearless in a broken world and think that they are representing Jesus?"[3] If God judges your love for your family, neighbors, friends, pastor, and coworkers by your prayers for them, what words might He use to describe your concern?

9. When my children were small, I recall sitting in church thinking of another mother's disciplined prayer life for her children. The Holy Spirit asked me: "Do you love your children that much?" I began to understand that my primary way of showing love for my children would be through my prayers.

Who could you show love to through your intercessory prayer?

Start here point

Reflecting His Love

Ruth and a college classmate did not get along. Ruth told me the story: "Others didn't know of our dislike for each other, but we both knew it. This went on for two years. I thought, *I haven't done anything; this is her fault, so I don't need to apologize.*

"Finally, tired of harboring wrong feelings, I prayed, *Lord, would You help me to love her?* I still did not love her, though, despite my prayer.

"One day the Spirit convicted me that I should apologize to her. I saw her across the gym, and I started toward her, wondering why I was doing it.

"But as soon as I said her name, I felt God's love cover me—from the top of my head down to my feet. When I asked her to forgive me, she began telling me all the things I had done wrong. Amazed, I thought, *There's another side to this!* We became friends and are still close friends today."

The moment Ruth did her part, God gave her an overflow of love. Producing the fruit of the Spirit is a cooperative effort between us and the Holy Spirit. It's as though our loving acts open the channel for His love to flow through us.

1. When a woman told me she didn't love her husband, I asked her what she would do differently if she did love him. She quickly responded, "I'd fold his clothes when I do the laundry." Why is God not likely to help her love her husband as long as she refuses to fold his clothes? Consider 2 John 6 and 1 Tim. 6:11.

2. Paul said, "The only thing that counts is faith expressing itself through love" (Gal. 5:6). How would the wife be expressing faith if she folded her husband's laundry?

3. Why could she not trust God to love her husband through her without this act of obedience?

4. One of the aspects of divine love is that it enjoys what it loves. Think of someone you know who enjoys you. Isn't the person's enjoyment of you one of the things that draws you to him or her? Compare this person's pleasure in you to how you feel about being around those who disapprove of you.

Do you believe someone who says he or she loves you but doesn't appear to enjoy being with you? To whom could you show the love of Christ by expressing your enjoyment of him or her?

5. Could it be that Jesus ate with the sinners because He wanted them to know He enjoyed them? Do you think it's possible to convince people we love them if we don't enjoy them?

6. One of the ways I knew my mother enjoyed me was her obvious interest in the details of my life. What are other ways we show people we enjoy them? Think of ways others effectively express their enjoyment in you.

God delights in us because He loves us. We love others by delighting in them. God will help us learn to delight in others if we ask Him.

Some time ago a friend made a few remarks on the phone about some people. She really had not intended to be critical. Yet, after we hung up I realized that I felt negative toward them, and I was going to have to try to have a ministry with this group. *It's not worth the effort,* I was tempted to think as negative thoughts rolled in.

As I went about my day, an amazing thing began to happen. God impressed a precious truth on my heart. It was as though He let me see these people as He did. I thought of our time together and knew the Holy Spirit would be there. Immediately I recognized that He would not be there to be critical of them but to uplift, encourage, comfort. His banner over them would be love (see Song of Sol. 2:4). As I thought of His love, the Spirit poured out into my heart His love for them.

7. One lady said that after reading in John 17:26 of Jesus' desire for us to love Him, she prayed for three years that she might love Jesus more. One day the Holy Spirit said, "If you love Jesus, you love every member of His Body."

We love Jesus no more than we love the member of His Body whom we love the least. Why would this be true? Consider 1 John 4:20-21.

8. What are some of the expressions the Bible uses that describe the love we ought to have for one another?
Rom. 12:10

Heb. 13:1

1 Pet. 1:22

1 Pet. 3:8

"To recognize that there is someone I do not love is to say to God, 'I do not love You enough to love that person.'"[4]

9. God is always pouring out His love. He loves the inconsiderate coworker, the salesperson at the door, the noisy people in the next apartment, the disappointing teacher, the rude clerk at the dress shop, the contractor who has cut down the row of trees we love, and the poky driver ahead of us. God loves, not tolerates, all of us at all times. List some whom you find it difficult to love, and invite the Holy Spirit to pour His love for them into your heart.

When God's Holy Spirit is poured into our hearts, His Holy Spirit becomes ours. Then we, too, are "gracious and compassionate, slow to anger and rich in love" (Ps. 145:8).

Memorize: "We rejoice in the hope of the glory of God. . . . And hope does not disappoint us, because God has poured out his love into our hearts by the Holy Spirit" (Rom. 5:2, 5).

Prayer: *Dear Lord, teach me to be completely humble and gentle, to patiently bear with others in love. I want to live a life of love, just as Christ loved me and gave himself up for me as a fragrant offering and sacrifice to You.*

Thank You for surrounding me with Your love. May all I do be done simply because I love You with all my heart and because nothing pleases me more than pleasing You. In Jesus' name I pray. Amen.

3

JOY

To DISCOVER JOY is to discover that God alone satisfies. Nothing else is even a close second. The psalmist exclaimed, "All my fountains are in you" (Ps. 87:7).

Nothing is more revealing about our inner man than what brings us joy. If our inner man is spiritually minded, we will desire the things the Spirit desires. Finding all our joys in God is the ultimate achievement of the Christian life.

Paul wrote from his prison cell, "Finally, my brothers, rejoice in the Lord!" (Phil. 3:1). We must learn to rejoice in God alone simply because of who He is, not because of what He promises or because of what He gives.

Portrait of Jesus' joy. What was the joy of Jesus? "'My food,' said Jesus, 'is to do the will of him who sent me and to finish his work'" (John 4:34). What satisfied Him was doing the will of His Father. To Jesus, joy was the result of doing everything for God's pleasure, and He wants that joy to be ours.

His joy in us. Several years ago I read a magazine article about Oprah Winfrey. Her fitness trainer, Bob Greene, related that one day he and Oprah were taking a long walk along Indiana's back roads when he asked her, "How often do you feel joy in your life?" She appeared caught off guard, so he restated the question—"When was the last time you experienced a joyful moment?"

"Oh, I'm trying to remember," she said. "I think it was 1985 when I was doing *The Color Purple*. I loved every moment of it." Bob said he dropped the subject.

The week I read that article, *Forbes* magazine came out listing the top 40 show biz celebrities. Heading the list was Oprah Winfrey. The blurb below her picture read, "Her uplifting chatter grossed $212 million this year."[1]

Those who look to their circumstances to give joy would think that if they had Oprah Winfrey's income, they would have lives of joy. I mentioned this article to a hairstylist in an elite neighborhood. She nodded and said, "I see these gals come in who live in million-dollar homes, and I can tell by their body language and what they say that they're not happy. They're empty. If we don't have happiness in ourselves, then we don't have any—because it doesn't come from outside."

I remembered that Jesus said that unless we partake of Him, "You have no life in you" (John 6:53), so I mentioned that without Jesus inside, we, too, are empty. We don't have a life without His life, but with His presence within, we can be full of joy.

Gaining His Joy

1. The Holy Spirit comes to give us joy. Notice how frequently the presence of the Holy Spirit is mentioned with that of joy.

Acts 13:52

Rom. 14:17

Rom. 15:13

1 Thess. 1:6

A friend commented, "When I was a teen I discovered that if I felt discouraged, I could go pray, and then I would feel better. Now I realize that it was because the Holy Spirit is a Spirit of joy. When I drew near to Him, I experienced His joy."

2. The joy Christ gives is a joy in the midst of suffering. One of the mind-sets that contributes to joy is looking past our circumstances. Even on the eve of the Crucifixion, Jesus comforted His disciples with "Let not your heart be troubled" (John 14:1, KJV).

"Happiness" comes from the same word as "happenings." When happenings change, so does happiness. The joy of the Lord, however, is a joy that no one can take from us (see John 16:22). Christ's joy remains despite burned casseroles, no promotions at work, and even poor health; it abounds under all conditions. In fact, the joy of the Lord is often the most evident in trying times. Consider 2 Cor. 8:2.

In his quaint way, John Bunyan described how he wrote *Pilgrim's Progress* in the Bedford dungeon: "So . . . I sat me down and wrote and wrote, because joy did make me write."[2]

3. It is this joy while suffering that most clearly distinguishes Christ's joy from the joy the world gives. What reasons for rejoicing in the midst of suffering are given in the following verses?

Rom. 5:3

James 1:2-3

1 Pet. 4:13

Acts 5:41

Because of such reasons, Paul could write that believers are "sorrowful, yet always rejoicing" (2 Cor. 6:10).

4. "Our greatest trouble may become our advantage, by entitling us to a new manner of the divine presence," stated E. E. Shelhammer. How true! Several weeks after my mother passed away, I decided to make her favorite orange cake. The last time I had fixed this recipe, I did it especially for her. Suddenly, standing at the kitchen table dumping ingredients, I felt a deep sadness. But it was only for a moment. *She's eating something so much better now!* The thought came with great joy.

Do you recall a time of great personal sorrow or struggle when joy of the Lord became your strength?

5. Shadrach, Meshach, and Abednego could in no way have anticipated the joy their severest trial would bring them—the joy of fellowshipping with the Son of God (see Dan. 3). Their furnace experience must have been a treasured memory, the time when their fellowship with God had been the closest. "In thy presence is fullness of joy" wrote the psalmist in Ps. 16:11 (KJV). Here's the paradox of our life in Christ: human sorrow can be overcome by joy in the Holy Spirit. See 2 Cor. 7:4.

6. Holy joy is often the most evident when we're in trying times. Yet the word translated "joy" in the New Testament does not involve a denial of reality. What combination of situations did Paul give in 2 Cor. 8:2? Without grace, what chance would there be of those occurring together?

7. The Holy Spirit's joy, enabling us to victoriously overcome difficult circumstances, will often be the fruit of the Spirit that reveals Christ to others. The Spirit-filled Christians in Acts were "praising God, and having favour with all the people" (2:47, KJV). Is there often a correlation between our Spirit-filled joyfulness and our influence upon the unconverted? Why? For a biblical example, see Acts 16:25-34.

8. "Count it all joy" when you fall into temptations (James 1:2, KJV). We can bear a trial with a spirit of stoical endurance, or we can look to the Lord to give us a spirit of victorious joy maintaining faith and confidence that God is in control. Why doesn't Satan want us to be joyful Christians? Consider Neh. 8:10.

9. Joy is always a source of strength. When we're joyful, we feel equal to anything; when we're depressed, everything's a burden. This is true in the spiritual life as well as the physical. Hannah Whitall Smith wrote that it seems, however, "as if many Christians thought that depression and discouragement are looked upon as very pi-

ous and humble frames of mind, and joy is considered to be a sort of spiritual bon-bon, only to be partaken of at rare and uncertain intervals."[3] It's no wonder that many Christians' spiritual lives wither. See Joel 1:12 and Deut. 28:47-48. What will happen to our spiritual lives if we fail to rejoice in the Lord?

10. What was it for which the Hebrew Christians were congratulated for taking joyfully? See Heb. 10:34

This is not a common reaction. Some lose their joy over spilled coffee on a new tablecloth. Christian joy transcends circumstances.

Reflecting His Joy

Find joy in what gave Jesus joy.

1. Jesus had one purpose for all He did: "I seek not to please myself but him who sent me" (John 5:30). "I always do what pleases him" (8:29).

What satisfied Jesus, according to John 4:34? Can you say that?

2. I learned the secret of having joy when I heard my mother say, "If I know that God is pleased with me, then let other things fall where they will—I am happy." When joy in our lives can be defined as doing what pleases God, we discover that our joy overflows.

Another time my mother said, "I'm thankful there are few times I don't feel like praising the Lord." To rejoice in the Lord is to receive all He allows in our lives with thanksgiving. Consider the importance of obeying the commands of 1 Thess. 5:16, 18, to having His joy.

3. A friend quit her job as a certified public accountant, believing God wanted her to devote herself to His service. Temporarily she did volunteer bookkeeping for her church. One day she walked into the church office and was asked to go to the courthouse to register the van. Unaccustomed to being handed such a menial task, she was tempted to feel resentment, but she related, "As soon as I yielded that immediate human response, I was filled with joy. My heart was as light as a feather as I drove away."

Complete this prayer with an unpleasant situation in your life: *Dear Lord, my highest joy is in pleasing You, so it doesn't matter if* _____. *If You're pleased with me and my attitude, that's enough.*

Have you experienced the joy of knowing in your spirit His whisper "I'm pleased with you"? The joy of His approval is beyond any earthly joy. The excitement of a new house, fame, money, and others' approval all seem trivial by comparison.

God asks, "Isn't My pleasure sufficient? Isn't it enough to know that I'm delighted with your attitude? Do you seek anything more than knowing I'm pleased?"

Oswald Chambers said, "What was the joy of Jesus? That He did the will of His Father, and He wants that joy to be ours."[4]

Start

Choose joy.

4. Frequently we're told to rejoice, as though it's something we can and should do regardless of how we feel. See Deut. 12:7, 18; 16:11; 1 Thess. 5:16.

5. Only a God of joy who gives us His presence continually could command us to rejoice always. What did David do to ensure that the leaders brought the ark to Jerusalem with joy? See 1 Chron. 15:16. Also see verse 25.

6. Notice that David appointed singers to sing joyful songs. Sometimes we need to determine to do what we would do if we felt joyful rather than allow circumstances to control how we feel and act. We may need to determine to praise as the psalmist did in Ps. 108. Notice the determination expressed in verses 1-3.

7. God gives us grace to receive His joy when we choose to do so. Some become bitter as they grow older; others whose lives are harder have a happy spirit. The difference rests in the inner choices of the heart.

I spoke with a friend I had not seen in years. She said, "I'm 74, and I work at Wal-Mart to pay expenses, but that's all right. I'm able and I enjoy it. I'm happy."

We can accept God's grace or choose to be discontent and unthankful. Do the inner choices of your heart generally make you a happy person?

8. Delighting in God's choices for us is a part of finding our joy in Him. Discontentment signals a failure to delight in the Lord. How serious is this in God's sight? Consider Deut. 28:47-48.

Partake of Jesus' life through the Word.

Oswald Chambers wrote, "The joy of Jesus is a miracle; it is not the outcome of my doing things or of my being good, but of my receiving the very nature of God."[5] One of the ways we do that is to take His words into our lives so that we become living expressions of His truth.

Years ago I began to take very literally the command "Fear God and keep his commandments, for this is the whole duty of man" (Eccles. 12:13). If fearing Him enough to keep His commands was my only duty, then I wanted all I did to be done in response to His Word. This new approach to life did not change what I did as much as it changed my motives for my actions and attitudes.

The amazing result was the overflowing joy I began experiencing. Jesus had said that if I abided in Him and His Word abided in me, He would give me His joy (John 15:10-11). I understood—and experienced—"fullness of joy" (Ps. 16:11, NKJV).

9. "Let the word of Christ dwell in you richly" (Col. 3:16). To have Christ's joy is to have His Word within. Jesus was God's Word expressed in a human body. See John 1:14.

As we take in His Word and become the living expression of that Word through obedience, His joy becomes our joy.

10. Have you noticed the joy that comes in spending time in the Word? Consider in Jer. 15:16 the connection between His Words and our joy.

Since His Word gives us joy, on the mornings when we awaken with a lack of joy, the cure may be to begin memorizing verses and filling our minds with Scripture. Try having verses on cards available to glance at while you get dressed or drive to work.

Memorize: "May the God of hope fill you with all joy and peace as you trust in him, so that you may overflow with hope by the power of the Holy Spirit" (Rom. 15:13).

Prayer: *Dear Lord, thank You for giving me a heart that delights in what You delight in, that calls pleasing You my highest joy. I don't care what You choose for me today—only let me go with the joy of Your presence. I ask this in Jesus' name. Amen.*

4

PEACE

PEACE IS THE INWARD REST the Holy Spirit gives. It refers to our inner tranquillity and poise we have as we look to Christ. The spirit of worry is gone, and we rest in an atmosphere of calm no matter what the day holds. Peace is a direct result of faith, because we're trusting that God is in control.

Portrait of Jesus' peace. When Gethsemane was almost in sight and Calvary was near, Jesus said, "Peace I leave with you; my peace I give you" (John 14:27). As the Prince of Peace, Jesus is qualified to bequeath His peace to His followers.

The peace He gives is the same peace He had in the midst of the Galilean storm and the calmness He experienced when He stood before His accusers. He whispers, "In me you may have peace. In this world you will have trouble. But take heart! I have overcome the world" (John 16:33).

His peace in us. "When I was in my upper teens, my mother became concerned about my college choice," a friend shared. "She wanted me to go to Bible college, but I wanted to accept a university scholarship. She was deeply concerned and praying. I was praying, too, but we were not in agreement.

"One day her countenance was completely different, and she seemed at peace about the situation. After I was in college—Bible college," he admitted with a grin, "I asked mother why she had stopped praying before the decision had been made.

"She said that she had totally committed her burden to God and that He had given her peace. She recognized that it was then His responsibility to direct me and not hers."

One of the clearest evidences of the Holy Spirit's presence is a peaceful spirit. It is in our daily situations that God wants us to experience His peace.

I received an E-mail from a friend who had just found a growth on her daughter's head alongside the incision from an operation to remove a malignant melanoma. She signed it, "Focusing on the Lord, receiving His perfect peace."

Let's consider what this peace is like and how we can manifest and bear more of this fruit of the Spirit.

Receive His Peace

Jesus said that He gives us peace "not as the world gives" (John 14:27, NKJV), so evidently the world gives a type of peace. However, it's a surface peace with no outer conflicts. It may be a temporary peace or a peace in the midst of prosperity or other pleasant circumstances.

Let's discuss some of the qualities that belong only to His peace.

1. Unlike the peace the world gives, this fruit of the Spirit is not dependent upon or altered by circumstances, because it's the "peace of God," and God is not disturbed by circumstances. How do the following verses state that the peace experienced by those who are filled with His Spirit is actually His peace?

John 14:27

Eph. 2:14

2. The timing of God's peace differs from that of the world. The peace the world gives comes after war, but Gideon heard "Peace!" before he entered the battle. See Judg. 6:11-24.

3. The peace the world gives comes after the desire is fulfilled, but God gives His peace to those who believe His promises. What signs of peace did Hannah show in 1 Sam. 1:17-18?

4. The peace of God is not passivity. Jesus was called the "Prince of Peace." Can you think of situations in which He was not passive?

5. His peace is not the Nirvana of the Buddhist nor that of the yoga instructors with their claim to calm the nerves. Sometimes a form of "stillness" is confused with the supernatural peace of God. If people are encouraged to abandon good works and simply to remain "still" before the Lord, they may mistakenly think they're experiencing God's peace. God's peace results from faith. See Isa. 26:3 and Rom. 5:1.

6. To the Hebrews, peace was not negative, but intensely positive. It was not freedom from trouble, but it involved everything that makes for our highest good. What are some of the wonderful effects mentioned in Isa. 32:17-18?

7. The peace of Christ does not include being able to live comfortably with evil. What breaks God's heart will break ours. Twice in Jeremiah (6:14-15 and 8:11-12) God warns against those whose conduct is not right in His sight while they say they have peace. Read these verses and consider why this made God so angry with them. Is He still angry when we can live comfortably with sin as though nothing is wrong?

Reflecting His Peace

1. *Delight in God's will.* "Acquaint now yourself with Him [agree with God and show yourself to be conformed to His will] and be at peace" (Job 22:21, AMP.).

Rather than delighting in God's will, some Christians are merely resigned to it. When trouble comes, they may at first resent the trouble but eventually resign themselves to the will of God. Resignation is better than rebellion, yet often when one says, "I'm resigned to it now," it means he or she is putting up with the inevitable. Such a person is not gladly submissive.

Joe Smalley, director of Athletes in Action in Europe, developed a brain tumor and faced suffering, pain, and death. During his illness he said, "I have come to see that this is God's plan for me. It is not His punishment; it is His beautiful plan for me. A difficult one, but a good one. I have even come to praise Him for it. This may seem difficult for some people to understand. People say, 'What about the children?' How sad for the children, but they are God's children first and foremost. God cares for His children."[1]

Mary met the annunciation with happy submission: "Behold the handmaid of the Lord; be it unto me according to thy word" (Luke 1:38, KJV). Is there any point of contention in your life against God's will? Any area in which you can't gladly say, *Be it unto me according to thy word*? If so, it's costing you the peace of God.

A lack of delight in God's will may show up as discontentment, which is not compatible with peace. "Bob said he has prayed and prayed for the rest and peace that I have," Alan said. "He's an architect for millionaires, and he sees their homes and wants to have what they have. Discontentment can easily destroy our peace because we don't delight in what God gives."

2. *Believe God attentively cares for every detail of your life.* We can have peace only if we delight in the Lord's will, no matter what that will may be. And we can delight in the Lord's will only if we truly believe both love and wisdom are behind all that comes to us.

How do the following verses teach that the One offering us peace is an all-powerful God who directs the universe and cares for every detail of our lives?

Matt. 10:29-31

1 Pet. 5:7

3. Write at least one Scripture passage that helps you believe God is performing His will in even the most difficult parts of your life.

4. *Thankfulness gives peace.* "Recently I was quite anxious about a particular, painful circumstance in my life," wrote Cynthia Heald in her book *Becoming a Woman of Freedom.* She said she prayed as she had never prayed before but remained anxious and unable to experience the peace of God.

As she meditated on Phil. 4:6-7 (wondering why it wasn't working), she realized that she was doing everything Paul said to do except to pray with thanksgiving. "To be honest, I couldn't think of anything I could really be thankful for in this situation. But Paul says to pray and ask with thanksgiving—the peace of God will follow."

As she began to pray with gratitude—thanking God for hearing her requests, for His love and understanding of her hurt, for His sovereignty and power—then and only then did she begin to know the peace of God, which transcends understanding.[2]

Anxiety should be a call to prayer and thanksgiving. Why do you think thankfulness frees us to trust?

5. *Refuse anxious thoughts!* Notice the phrase "Do not be anxious about anything" in Phil. 4:6-7. It covers all possible reasons for anxious thoughts. What are some things we can do that will help us to refuse anxious thoughts?

6. In John 14:1, 27, Jesus commands us not to be troubled or afraid. Every time we yield to anxiety or fear, we're failing to please Him. What are our anxieties saying to Him about His care for us?

7. What role does disciplining our anxious thoughts play in receiving God's peace? Consider the words of Jesus and Paul:

"Peace I leave with you. . . . Let not your heart be troubled" (John 14:27, NKJV).

"Let the peace of Christ rule in your hearts" (Col. 3:15).

8. *Believe God.* David wrote in Ps. 26:1, "I have trusted in the LORD without wavering." To the degree that we can say, "I'm trusting in the Lord without wavering," we have peace.

Three times Jesus rebuked the disciples for their little faith. Yet in each case we would have thought that anxiety would have been the natural, maybe even the appropriate, response. What was the problem in Matt. 8:24-26?

9. Would you tell someone in the middle of a storm, when the waves are covering their boat, that their anxiety indicates little faith? Yet Jesus knew that with Him on board, there was no way they could be harmed. Even in our storms we're invited to rest in quiet confidence. What storm are you experiencing that could be an occasion of receiving God's peace?

10. What was Peter's condition in Matt. 14:29-31 that indicated to Jesus that he lacked faith?

Even when we're about to sink, peace comes simply by our looking to Jesus.

11. What was the occasion in Matt. 16:8-10 that prompted Jesus to speak of their little faith?

12. Here Jesus referred them to past experiences in which He had supplied their needs as a reason they should trust Him now. Often reviewing past help from God restores our peace. Recall a time God gave you peace when you trusted Him.

A friend told me that her college-age son called early one semester saying the classes he needed were filled. As she envisioned another year of college and another

$8,000, her fear began to mount. The next morning, though, she read what she had written in her prayer journal when John was making choices about college and classes. She had asked God to direct him in the right path.

"As I read what I had written and remembered that I had asked God to direct, I believed that God was directing. If John had to drop out, then that was God's will for him." That confidence gave her peace, and she rested in God's care for her son. He called the next week saying he had been able to get the classes he needed after all.

13. *Spend time in His presence.* When Martha criticized her sister, Mary stayed in Jesus' presence until the enemies of her peace were silenced. See Luke 10:38-42.

Jesus will defend those who look to Him. See Ps. 34:5.

14. Often we don't have the peace of God because we're occupying our minds with things that make us doubt. What's the connection between faith and peace given in Rom. 15:13?

15. *Live the Word.* According to the following verses, what connection is there between peace and obeying His words?

Isa. 48:18

Ps. 119:165

16. *Let peace be your guide.* "Let the peace of Christ rule in your hearts" (Col. 3:15). The word "rule" is a verb used of the umpire whose decision settled any matter of dispute. If the peace of Christ is the umpire in our hearts, then when we feel pulled in two directions, peace is to be the arbiter. If we accept its decision, we can't go wrong.

Read this verse in *The Amplified Bible:* "And let the peace (soul harmony which comes) from Christ rule (act as umpire continually) in your hearts [deciding and settling with finality all questions that arise in your minds, in that peaceful state] to which as [members of Christ's] one body you were also called [to live]. And be thankful (appreciative), [giving praise to God always]."

Which thought in this verse means the most to you?

17. What does God promise in Isa. 60:17?

18. *Recognize that peace is a gift of God.* We receive peace by faith. In fact, ceasing our own efforts and looking to God to give us peace is the secret. Write two insights about peace you find in 2 Thess. 3:16.

19. What price was paid for you to have the gift of peace? See Isa. 53:5

20. *Be filled with the God of peace.* The literal translation of 1 Thess. 5:23 is "the God of peace himself sanctify you wholly" (author's paraphrase). It expresses in the most emphatic way that God himself is the Author of our sanctification. He makes us holy by filling us with himself.

To be filled with the Holy Spirit is to be filled with the God of peace. We don't fill ourselves with peace—rather, it's the work of the Spirit in response to our faith and obedience.

Justification brings us peace with God; sanctification brings into our spirit the abiding presence of the God of peace himself. True peace is then nothing less than the indwelling of His tranquillity.

Have you trusted the God of peace to fill you with himself so others will see His peace in you?

Memorize: "The meek . . . shall delight themselves in the abundance of peace" (Ps. 37:11, KJV).

Prayer: *Dear Lord, I praise You for the peace that comes as I wholly surrender and trust You. It is nothing less than the very heart of Christ resting in my heart and imparting to me the very same peace He had when He faced the prospect of the garden and the Cross. Thank You for giving me grace to refuse to be anxious as I bring everything to You in prayer and praise. In Jesus' name. Amen.*

5

PATIENCE

PATIENCE ENABLES US to respond to frustrating circumstances with grace and self-control. It's not merely a personality trait, but a by-product of the presence of the Holy Spirit in our lives.

Patience, also translated as "long-suffering," means to keep good-natured under provocation. It implies a forgiving spirit and a willingness to pass over, or even forget, wrongs inflicted by others. Long-suffering is slow to suspect wrong, slower to blame others, and slower still to resent the wrong.

Portrait of Jesus' patience. In Matt. 5:39, Jesus taught that when caustic words are said, we're not to resist. When "He was oppressed and afflicted, yet he did not open his mouth; he was led like a lamb to the slaughter, and as a sheep before her shearers is silent, so he did not open his mouth" (Isa. 53:7).

With His presence sustaining us, we, too, are expected to "not repay evil with evil or insult with insult, but with blessing, because to this you were called so that you may inherit a blessing" (1 Pet. 3:9).

His patience in us. "Love is patient," we studied in our neighborhood Bible study. Carol had never thought of love as being patient. "Just think of all of the chances there are to show impatience during the day," she said. "First, someone's late for breakfast . . ."

There are many occasions throughout our day that we choose to either respond with the patience the Holy Spirit provides or grieve Him by responding out of our own impulsive spirit. Paul wrote in that same chapter, "Love never fails" (1 Cor. 13:8). As we continually walk in the Spirit, He teaches us to remain good-natured, even under provocation.

In his book *Pure in Heart*, W. E. Sangster tells that his father watched as a Salvation Army preacher was struck by a half-drunken man. As the preacher fell, he struck his head against the curb with such force that everyone thought he was dead. He struggled to his feet, looked at the man who had struck him, said, "God bless you," and resumed his address.[1]

That's patience! But it's also patience when the children spill their orange juice or our boss criticizes our best efforts and refuses to give us a promotion—and we're still full of love.

The Holy Spirit is love, and when our spirits are controlled by His Spirit, we'll be true expressions of His love. If we continually walk in the Spirit, we have all the fruit of the Spirit—including patience. As we depend upon the Spirit, He'll help us grow in our ability to have a patient spirit.

Reflections on Patience

The pain of thousands of families would disappear if impatience were conquered. If excused, however, it jeopardizes the salvation of the family.

Impatience and irritability are frequent failings in the home. "When I was young," a friend told us, "I overheard a father in our church angrily scold his children. I thought, 'Tonight when we go to church, you may testify, but I won't believe you have what you say.'"

1. Our patience—or lack of it—may be the most telling thing about the effectiveness of our Christian testimony. Unbelievers will want to use our impatience as an excuse to doubt our sincerity. Are they justified in doing this? Notice the phrase "live a life worthy" in connection with patience in Eph. 4:1-2 and Col. 1:10-11.

2. In 2 Cor. 6:4-6 and 2 Tim. 3:10, Paul says patience is one of the proofs of real discipleship.

3. Imagine being in Jerusalem when Jesus was being tried and seeing His face red with anger, hearing Him respond bitterly to the abuse of His enemies. What would this do to your concept of Him as the Spirit of love?

4. Read in 1 Pet. 2:21-23 Christ's response when mistreated.

Perhaps nothing makes us seem more perfect than a patient spirit. "But let patience have her perfect work, that ye may be perfect and entire, wanting nothing" (James 1:4, KJV).

Marilyn said she noticed that she set the tone for her family on Sunday mornings. "When I feel rushed and out-of-sorts because we're going to be late for church, our whole family is grumpy. But when I'm calm and happy, the whole family seems to absorb my contentment."

5. Impatience perpetuates itself. If we as parents impatiently respond to our children, their sunny dispositions disappear in a minute. A half dozen quarrels later, we find we're punishing the children for their bad attitudes! Consider how Prov. 15:18 applies to our homes.

6. Can you recall a time when a patient answer calmed a quarrel?

7. A reproof given to vent an impatient spirit is one thing; a reproof given to lovingly discipline a child is another. The former is an act of disobedience; the latter is an act of obedience to God. The former will help ruin your child; the latter will help save him or her. Can you think of at least two reasons why impatience harms a child?

_____

One of Satan's subtle plans is to make us view our impatience as being of slight importance, hardly worthy of our concern. When the Spirit reproves us, it's natural to excuse our impatience by thinking, "I had good reason to be upset."

Is our patience of any value if it appears only when there are no grounds for impatience? The beauty of the real thing is in that it is most evident when there are great reasons for impatience.

8. What situations frequently give you opportunity to demonstrate this fruit of the Spirit?

9. Notice the benefits named in the following verses in Proverbs to those who are "slow to become angry" (James 1:19).

14:29

16:32

19:11

10. Also notice a few of the warnings given in Proverbs to those who are "soon angry."

14:17

19:19

22:24-25

Reflecting His Patience

Satan has inspired the idea that it's best to ventilate our feelings—that if we're angry, suppression will only cause more damage. Like all his inspirations, this is untrue—you might as well tell a lie to make yourself more truthful.

An impatient spirit thrives on exercise. Each frown indulged and each impatient remark will increase the power of the impatient spirit. Every time you remain patient when severely tempted, you strengthen this grace.

David vented his feelings, but he vented them to God. God is big enough and wise enough to handle our feelings. He can even help us to understand why we respond impatiently.

1. It's important to very carefully guard our thoughts about the one who is a trial to us. If we insist on entertain-

ing ourselves with memories of his or her unkindness, our impatience will be well nourished. Read 1 Cor. 13:4-7, thinking of the one who causes you the most trouble, and notice how your thoughts toward that person are softened.

What impact do you think guarding your thoughts has on your ability to be patient?

2. Our patience with others will be greatly strengthened by reflecting on the patience of God with us. When we're tempted to be upset over some little things we need not have noticed, let's recall God's patience with us. How would you describe His patience as described in Rom. 2:4 and 1 Tim. 1:16?

3. Avoid loud, sharp tones of voice when exasperated. Our own words have a tremendous power to mold our spirits. If we wait until we're certain something has to be said and then say it slowly and gently, our own spirits as well as the spirits of those around us will be calmed. See Prov. 15:1.

4. If we've lapsed into the habit of overreacting or of speaking sharply, the Holy Spirit will help us modify our behavior. A minister said that when he's tempted to feel great irritation, he looks up and claims the patience and gentleness of Christ. We look to Him and are suddenly enabled to deal with a troublesome situation calmly and kindly. Write Phil. 4:13, inserting the words "even be patient."

5. Impatience and irritability are among our most common temptations. Would you agree with the one who said, "There's no more sure sign of a disciplined mind than a habit of tolerance and patience"? Why or why not?

6. What verbs in the following verses are used to describe what we're to do with anger?

Ps. 37:8

Eph. 4:31

Col. 3:8

7. When conversation would tend to cause friction, change the subject unless the topic is something that needs to be discussed. Indeed, the underlying causes of the provocation may need to be discussed in order for you to have a healthy relationship. Often when provoked, we're so fearful of the emotions that would arise and the intensity of our response, that we hesitate to deal with the issues. The intensity may be a clue that the topic is something that needs to be dealt with. The key, though, is to do only what the Holy Spirit directs you to do. As you focus on Him, He will give you both the patience and the guidance you need at each moment.

If avoiding the conflict is not possible or wise, listen quietly while you keep looking to Jesus. Consider how He would respond. Remember the last phrase of 1 Cor. 2:16.

8. God's promises are failures if He cannot keep us from impatience. As always, the work God requires of us is faith—a faith that looks to Him to provide grace to do His will. "God's work . . . is by faith" (1 Tim. 1:4). None of the fruit of the Spirit can be done in our own strength. What would we be tempted to do if we could do it without the help of the Spirit? See Eph. 2:9.

9. God does not take away our ability to become impatient. We still have a choice between responding to a difficulty with love or anger. The keeping power of God is predicated on our cooperation.

He keeps no one holy who does not persistently avoid all that's unholy. Just as He can't keep our thoughts pure if we insist on looking at impure pictures or reading matter, so God will not keep us in perfect patience if we keep on yielding to impatience.

Make it a habit never to reply instantly when you're tempted to be annoyed. If any reply is needed, trust the Holy Spirit to give you the right thing to say. This will give a death blow to impatience. See James 1:19-20.

10. Pastor Dennis Eenigenburg's mother modeled a patient spirit when her son brought home a note from his elementary school teacher stating he had spoken disrespectfully to his teacher. Many mothers would have been tempted to drop a verbal guillotine on the child's neck.

Instead, she read the note, stood there with tears in her eyes, and then led him to her bedroom. Dennis was expecting a well-deserved spanking, but what he got was far more effective. "She had me kneel down with her as she prayed and asked the Lord for wisdom to guide her son, and as she prayed, she cried. I was deeply moved. If my behavior was that important to her, I knew I had to change. No spanking I ever received had as much impact as kneeling next to my praying mother."[2]

This woman saw a deeper need and because she loved her son she responded to that.

"For the wrath of man worketh not the righteousness of God" (James 1:20, KJV). Why is discipline administered in anger usually ineffective?

11. Consider how this mother's love for her son caused her to refrain from reacting merely to the issue of the moment. Do you think impatience indicates a lack of love?

"Love endures long and is patient and kind" (1 Cor. 13:4, AMP.). "This love . . . is slow to lose patience—it looks for a way of being constructive" (PHILLIPS). Love tends to make us gentle, tender, and affectionate.

12. Insist on saying and doing nothing that you would not say or do if you saw Jesus sitting beside you. Then, by acts of kindness and a sweet spirit, follow up wrongs that have been done to you. See 1 Pet. 3:9.

Memorize: "Be completely humble and gentle; be patient, bearing with one another in love" (Eph. 4:2).

Prayer: *Dear Lord, I ask You to fill me with the knowledge of Your will in order that I may live a life worthy of You and please You in every way. Strengthen me with all power according to Your glorious might so that I may have great endurance and patience and joyfully give thanks to the Father. I pray this in the name of Jesus. Amen.*
                        —Prayer adapted from Col. 1:9-12

6

KINDNE**ss**

KINDNESS IS THE SWEET DISPOSITION that makes others feel at ease with us and causes us to shrink from hurting another. It causes our spirit to be eager to give whatever may be necessary—a word of recognition, a listening ear, affirmation. We instinctively love to do others good, even if it means we have to give up our rights.

The Old Testament word "loving-kindness" is derived from a Hebrew word meaning "to bend or bow oneself," which indicates a gracious, humble spirit.

Portrait of Jesus' kindness. "Let the little children come to me, and do not hinder them" (Matt. 19:14). Jesus did not say, "Force the little children to come to me." The implication is that the children were *eager* to crawl up on His lap and would come unless prevented.

Both children and adults are drawn to a genuinely kind spirit. Evidently the sinners who wanted to join Jesus for dinner at Matthew's house delighted in being with Him (see Matt. 9:10). The Pharisees, who valued the letter of the Law more than love, were never troubled with sinners wanting to come to their celebrations.

His kindness in us. One day when our daughter Arla was about nine years old, I asked her to dust the furniture. Every little bit she was crying or complaining. First, she bumped her head and then her arm. Next, she got a splinter in her hand, and then she couldn't remember which shelves she had dusted. Frustrated with her, I threatened to spank if she didn't quit complaining.

Finally, I silently sighed, *Jesus, what would You do with a child like this?*

Immediately these words came to my mind: "I'd spend a lot of time with her."

Amazed that God had actually seemed to respond, I went to Arla, and, instead of scolding her and then walking away as I had been doing, I stayed with her, trying to speak kindly as I knew Jesus would while she did her work. Amazingly, her attitude brightened, and she was happy and talkative.

The lady in Prov. 31 "opens her mouth with wisdom, and on her tongue is the law of kindness" (v. 26, NKJV). What a law to try to continually enforce on ourselves!

Often we react unkindly rather than fleeing to the One who wants to give us His thoughts, His reactions. Because we have access to the mind of Christ, we don't need to respond out of our human weakness.

"What is the single quality that strikes you most about Christ?" one pastor frequently asks those who come to him in trouble. He reports that almost without exception they cite His understanding, tenderness, or kindness.

As His image-bearers we, too, are to be known as those who take time to care. To be kind is to be loving in the brief contacts of life.

Bob Benson told of an electrician nicknamed "Motormouth" because he was such a talker. He always had a smile and a ready answer to any question. But one day Motormouth shot himself.

Benson wrote, "I'd asked him lots of times how he was doing, but I guess I had never asked him in a way that made him want to tell me. Life in a way is like those electric bumper cars at the amusement park. We just run at each other and smile and bump and away we go."[1]

Kindness is time-consuming. It uses up time we could spend on ourselves. It takes time to visit people, to do small favors, to listen to the heartaches and heart longings of others, to run errands for them, to help them with their work, to write them letters, to give of our time and strength to brighten their lives.

Sometimes, though, kindness requires almost no time—just a sincere interest in others. It's a matter of awareness and sensitivity that are very simple in nature. A smile. A hug. A sharing.

Someone has said that if you wanted to express Christianity in one English word, you would use the word "kindness." In the early centuries, pagans confused the words "kindly" and "Christ," because the Greek words were so much alike, but, as Tertullian remarked, they were so close in meaning that no harm was done by the confusion.

Reflections on Kindness

"Do not grieve the Holy Spirit of God. . . . Be kind and compassionate to one another, forgiving each other" (Eph. 4:30, 32). When we're unkind, the Holy Spirit within us is grieved.

1. Kindness keeps us from being judgmental and critical. A church leader observed, "Religious people are an unkind lot." Often people who strictly observe religious codes are strangely hard and unfeeling. This was one aspect of the sin of the Pharisees. What warning did Jesus give in Matt. 12:7?

2. Why do you think the temptation to unkindness is so great to those who strictly observe God's law?

3. It's easy to lose sympathy with those who have failed to keep what we believe to be God's standard for us. We're tempted to become censorious and find it hard to adopt any attitude that seems to lessen the seriousness of what we consider to be sin. We think a harsh attitude will

bring a change, but what will actually work far more effectively? According to Rom. 2:4, what does kindness do?

4. "And the Lord turned and looked straight at Peter. . . . And he went outside and wept bitterly" (Luke 22:61-62). Do you think there was any rebuke in His look that said, "How dare you do such a thing?" What expression do you think there was in His look?

5. Do you think when we consider others to be unworthy of our kindness, tolerance, and patience, that our attitude toward them is interpreted by God as contempt for His kindness? Reread Rom. 2:4. ·

6. When we fail to show kindness, often a barrier goes up—not only to us, but also to the Holy Spirit. A judgmental attitude can hinder others from responding to Christ. Our words should prepare the way for the Holy Spirit—not make it more difficult for the Holy Spirit to be heard.

Someone has said, "I'd rather err in mercy than in judgment." Those are the kind of people we like to be around. Why is it that when certain people always believe in us and are always kind, we try much harder to please them than if we're constantly feeling their criticism?

7. Is there someone who might be hindered in responding to the Holy Spirit because he or she feels your disapproval?

A pastor said that God told him to extend his hand in warm fellowship to another. He objected: *But, Lord—if I do, he'll think I have confidence in him.*

God said, "Guard your spirit, and let Me take care of the other person. Divine love is very sensitive to anything that would disrupt fellowship."

8. To have the mind of Christ so that we have His discernment, we must have the same purpose as He had. In John 12:47 what did Jesus state was *not* the reason He came into the world?

9. If our goal is not to judge, but to save, what differences will that make in our thoughts, attitudes, and words? Notice that a judgmental attitude hinders our seeing others correctly. See Matt. 7:1-3, 5.

10. Nothing has drawing power like undeserved love expressed through kindness. Nancy had wandered from Christ's teaching. She frequently heard, "You should go to church." Such talk irritated her. After she returned to God, I asked her what had brought her back.

She responded, "I began to hear God say, 'I love you.'"

Jesus said, "If I be lifted up, I'll draw all people unto me" (John 12:32, author's paraphrase). His being lifted up refers to His death on the Cross. Seeing Jesus on the Cross is seeing His greatest expression of loving-kindness. Our kindness will do more than anything else to convince others of their spiritual need.

Because God has been gracious toward us, we should treat everyone with kindness. What does Luke 6:35-36 specifically mention we should do because of God's kindness?

Start Here Sept 2019

Reflecting His Kindness

To be kind is to be loving in our brief contacts with others. Because God is love, there is no stronger power in the universe than love, so even transient contacts that express kindness are powerful.

But have you ever thought, "I don't feel like being kind"? Feeling follows obedience. If we do our part, God will give us His love for others.

1. When we want God to love others through us, we often must first obediently do whatever we can. If we offer time, effort, or money, the desire to be kind will follow. Apply Matt. 6:21 to this concept.

2. In her book *With My Whole Heart,* Karen Mains tells of a discipline she has that reminds her to maintain a kind spirit. It involves a phrase she derived from an old prayer: "Christ betwixt thee and me." She writes, "I breathe the words 'Christ betwixt thee and me' when I grow impatient with the phone caller who is talking too long, with the difficult personality who is taxing my resources, with the cranky child. . . . I breathe the prayer, then see the form of Christ between me and the one to whom I am speaking."

She asks herself, "How would He respond to this one? What words would He choose? How would He touch? What kind of concern would He show?" Then she does whatever is closest to what she thinks Christ would do.[2]

Think of at least two situations in which such a discipline would help you to be kind.

3. Prayer is a powerful tool to use when we find we're unable to respond with kindness in our own strength. We look to Christ and pray, *Dear Lord, what are You thinking about this one?* and often find we suddenly possess a fresh love and understanding that enable us to deal kindly with a troublesome situation.

Kindness is one of the results of keeping in step with the Spirit. Read Gal. 5:22-25.

4. Also, be willing to pray for the one who has hurt you. That was Job's deliverance. God told Job to pray for those three miserable comforters. See Job 42:10. What happened then?

5. I once knew a man who had been wronged. During this time he hurt deeply, but the Lord impressed him to pray for the man who had wronged him. He was to pray that he would be effective in his ministry. The miracle that took place was that the bitterness against that man dissolved.

Turn over any injustice to God; don't insist on paying back the wrong—that's God's department. In fact, look for ways to do the person good. What instructions did Jesus give in Matt. 5:44?

6. Be alert to new ways to show kindness. What applications can you make from the following Old Testament verses?

Lev. 19:33-34

Ps. 112:5

7. A lady I sat beside on an airplane shared what she believed to have been a vision from God. She said she saw the back of Jesus, and she told God she wanted to see Jesus' face. When Jesus turned toward her, she realized that His face appeared differently to different people. To some He was the face of a disliked mother-in-law, to others a person they befriended. She recognized that the way the Christian treats another is the way he or she treats Christ.

See Matt. 25:40, 45, and consider the possible truth in her vision.

8. We should see all our actions and reactions to others as though they are done to the Lord. See Num. 5:6.

9. When we love others with the love of Christ, we will want to share our lives with them. Paul showed this aspect of love in 1 Thess. 2:8. Do people have a right to think we don't truly love them when we're not willing to spend time doing what they enjoy? Why or why not?

10. The lady of Prov. 31:26 had the law of kindness on her lips. She had a law—only kind words would pass from her lips. My mother had that law on her lips. I grew up in a home in which the minister was never criticized, those who had wronged us were excused, and people were not condemned. I've heard my mother say, "A temptation to think evil of someone will come to me, and I'll say, 'No, no, no.'" How important is guarding our thoughts the secret to having a loving spirit and consistently saying kind words?

11. If we guard our thoughts, our words and actions will be right. "Let the wicked forsake his way, and the unrighteous man his thoughts" (Isa. 55:7, NASB). It takes no more than wrong thoughts to make us unrighteous in God's eyes.

What kinds of things are we to think on, according to Phil. 4:8?

12. One sure way to lose the sense of God's presence is to speak unkind words about another. David states this in Ps. 15 in response to "LORD, who may dwell in your sanctuary?" What is his answer in verse 3? Why do we move out of God's presence when we begin casting slurs?

13. Being willing to gather additional information often enables us to respond with kindness. This can be a surprising experience. A man was riding on a train when a father and several children got on. The children began acting rather rowdy. The man saw that the father appeared oblivious to the disturbance his children were causing. He could take it no longer and turned to the man and said, "Your children are certainly causing a disturbance."

The man looked up rather startled and said, "Oh, I'm sorry. You see, my wife just passed away, and I hadn't noticed."[3]

Take time to listen to the person's side of the story. It doesn't mean you will think he or she is right, but if you can understand why the person is acting that way, your response will often be tempered with more love.

14. How do we show kindness? First, we must feel loving toward the person. This may require that we spend time praying until the love and concern we feel is God's love and concern. Our overtures—phone calls, letters, conversations—should result from love for the person and our confidence in Christ. If our confidence is in our own efforts, we often look at the results and say, "He [She] doesn't seem to be helped." When we're concerned enough about our friends to show them kindness because of Christ's love,

then God can use us. God said, "I led them with cords of human kindness, with ties of love" (Hos. 11:4). Notice the use of the word "human." Who might be some people God would want to draw to himself through your kindness?

Memorize: "Therefore, as God's chosen people, holy and dearly loved, clothe yourselves with compassion, kindness, humility, gentleness and patience" (Col. 3:12).

Prayer: *Thank You, dear Lord, for drawing me to You with loving-kindness. Give me the grace to express this same kindness to my family and friends so they will see You in me. In Jesus' name I pray. Amen.*

7

GOODNEſſ

GOODNESS is the perpetual desire to do good to others to the utmost of our ability. But all this must spring from a good heart—a heart with pure motives.

"A good person produces good words from a good heart" (Matt. 12:35, NLT). Goodness is always living for others and never seeking our own advantage. If we possess the fruit of goodness, we will be both generous and guileless—without hypocrisy. We will be what we appear to be.

Portrait of Jesus' goodness. "Jesus of Nazareth . . . went around doing good" (Acts 10:38). His life defines goodness. He was continually sensitive to how He might meet the needs of those around Him, and then He met those needs generously. He didn't just barely provide enough for the hungry 5,000, but He included a whole basket of leftovers for each of the 12 disciples who had assisted Him.

His goodness in us. A dear friend with whom I wanted to share God's love called. "I've just had surgery and the pain is unbearable. Will you pray for me?" I was happy for her request, because I had decided to spend the day in prayer and fasting. While praying, I thought of preparing our favorite tuna casserole for her family. "All the ingredients are in the kitchen," the Lord reminded me.

To my shame, I admit that I stuck to praying—surely God didn't have a better work for me to do than prayer! The next day the friend shared how angry her husband was that he had had to prepare dinner.

Being good is a matter of being sensitive to the promptings God gives. His promptings always harmonize with His Word. I realized this when I later read, "Is not this the kind of fasting I have chosen: . . . Is it not to share your food with the hungry?" (Isa. 58:6-7).

If we do what He calls "good," when we're finished we can hear His whisper, "Well done, good and faithful servant!" (Matt. 25:23).

"Why do you call me good?" Jesus said. "No one is good—except God" (Mark 10:18). I think we can extend that to mean that our deeds are not good unless they're the deeds God wants us to do.

Charles Spurgeon said, "No work can be good unless it is commanded of God. . . . The Pharisee said he tithed mint, anise, and cummin; could he prove that God commanded him to tithe his mint, his anise, and his cummin? Perhaps not. He said he fasted so many times a week; could he prove that God told him to fast? If not, his fasting was no obedience. If I do a thing that I am not commanded to do, I do not obey in doing it."[1]

The test of goodness is not by how we keep rules, but by how Christ-centered we are. Let's first contemplate God's goodness to gain an idea of how His goodness will look when Christ expresses His goodness through us. Then we'll consider guides to reflecting His goodness.

Reflections on God's Goodness

Goodness describes God's constant desire to communicate good to all His creation. It's one aspect of love, but His love is limited to those capable of receiving love. God's goodness, though, applies to the whole creation. "God saw all that he had made, and it was very good" (Gen. 1:31). Not a sparrow is forgotten before God (see Luke 12:6).

1. How does Ps. 145:9 suggest that He is always seeking to promote the happiness of all He created?

2. The psalmist seemed to take delight in meditating on the goodness of God. See Pss. 23:6; 31:19; 145:7.

3. Because His desire to do good to us is constant, He doesn't do good sometimes and bad other times. What does He promise in Jer. 32:40?

Even when things are going "bad," that does not mean God has stopped doing good. It means He's rearranging things to do us more good if we'll go on loving and trusting Him.

"The LORD will indeed give what is good" (Ps. 85:12). This is true even when we would not define what is happening as good. He knows how to bring good out of any situation.

4. God will not permit anything to happen to us utterly incapable of doing us good. If it were possible to conceive anything out of which infinite wisdom could not bring good, God would not allow it.

What do the following verses teach about the goodness of God in all circumstances?

Rom. 8:28

Ps. 84:11

Ps. 119:67, 71

Isa. 38:17

5. John Piper in *The Pleasures of God* wrote, "If an enemy is temporarily given the upper hand, we can say, straight into the muzzle of the gun, 'You mean evil against me, but God means it for good'" (Gen. 50:20).[2] Because God is sovereign and has promised not to turn His goodness away from us, what are we promised in Rom. 8:35-37?

God always wants to do us good, because He loves us. He has no hidden motive or agenda that makes it only appear that He's doing us good.

6. Even though the psalmist may have been temporarily unable to see evidences of God's goodness, of what was he confident? See Ps. 27:13. Such faith pleases God.

7. But God's promise of goodness is greater yet. Not only does He promise to do us good continually, but He's *eager* to do us good.

Jer. 32:41

Deut. 30:9

8. "Surely goodness and mercy shall follow me" (Ps. 23:6, KJV). The Hebrew word for "follow" means to "run after" or to "chase." God is *pursuing* us with goodness and mercy! No wonder the psalmist seemed to take delight in meditating on the goodness of God. What do the following verses say to you about the goodness of God?

Ps. 31:19

Ps. 145:7

"The earth is full of the goodness of the Lord" (Ps. 33:5, KJV). "Oh that men would praise the Lord for his goodness" (107:8, 15, 31, KJV). Think of at least three ways God has shown His goodness to you. Praise Him!

Reflecting His Goodness

1. The Holy Spirit provides a goodness "in the inward parts," making us transparent or guileless.

W. E. Sangster in his book *Pure in Heart* describes one who is guileless: "He does not aim to use you, as so many use their friends. He loves you—and for yourself alone. He is not mentally fitting you into his scheme. You are not just an actor in a play of which he is the central character. Loving you with a God-like love, he has but one thought: how he can help you."[3]

How does a delight in pleasing God protect us from subtle pretentiousness, an insincere appearance of doing good?

2. Consider how much simpler it is when our goal is simply as that of Jesus, who said, "I seek not to please myself but him who sent me" (John 5:30). We're not constantly calculating our chances of achieving what we want or always wondering how to manage in order to keep ahead of others.

Instead, we have but one ambition—to please the Lord. If we are uncertain at times what that will is, we know to be quiet and wait. When we know His will we accept it joyfully. See this attitude in Ps. 40:8.

3. Jesus was without guile. He did not aim to use others for His own purposes. He had but one thought: "How does My Father want Me to help others?"

The one who is without guile is able to excuse others' faults. "She's had a hard time in life," or "She didn't realize how wrong it was." Such phrases come naturally to those who think like Christ. A part of having the fruit of goodness is be willing to see the goodness in others. Paul wrote an astounding phrase to the Romans. See Rom. 15:14. Why is it difficult to be willing to see the goodness in others?

I recall a lesson God taught me when someone made some cutting remarks to me. Struggling to have a right response, I sent an SOS to God: *Please, Lord—give me a verse!* I got up from the table where we were sitting and walked over to the kitchen cabinet and saw these words of Paul, which I had taped there earlier: "And I myself also am persuaded of you, my brethren, that ye also are full of goodness" (Rom. 15:14, KJV). I knew God was saying, "Believe she is full of goodness." My spirit was not to be critical. Later when I understood the pressures she was under; I understood the reason for her sharp words. God knew that, and the mind of Christ said to believe good.

4. We should be "always slow to expose, always eager to believe the best, always hopeful" (1 Cor. 13:5, MOFFATT). Can you think of an example of any of these aspects of goodness in Christ?

5. If we possess the fruit of goodness, we'll be generous. In one of Jesus' parables (Matt. 20:1-16), a laborer complained because the landowner did not pay him more than He paid those who had been hired later. The landowner responded, "Don't I have the right to do what I want with my own money? Or are you envious because I am generous?" The Greek word for "generous" is the word commonly translated as "good."

What is the reward of the generous? See Ps. 112:5 and Luke 6:38.

6. To be truly generous is to give freely without hoping for personal gain. In a Midwestern university, students

were each asked to bring a dime to class. Then they were told, "People are starving in India because of a plague. If you'd like to help them, put the dime in an envelope and write on it, 'India.' A local family needs groceries. If you want to help these people, mark your envelope, 'Poor family.' Now, we don't have a copier accessible to the students. If you want to help buy a photocopier, mark your envelope, 'Copier.'" Eighty percent of the donated money went to a photocopy machine.

Think of time, money, or gifts you gave in the last month. Did you give without hoping for personal gain? Write three insights from Matt. 5:46—6:4 concerning generosity.

7. A speaker took a week's retreat during which she was alone in silence, prayer, and fasting, putting herself aside to listen to the Lord. In the quiet of that week, she felt impressed not to take honoraria for her scheduled meetings the next year. With the bills of two children in college, it was difficult, but she was obedient.

The first time she spoke knowing she would receive no money for her four days away from home, she stood on the platform, and her heart began to sing the words "To God! To God!"

Can you think of something that you have done, or can do, that would be solely to the glory of God?

8. If we possess the fruit of goodness, we might at times appear stern. Occasionally goodness, even the goodness of God, necessarily appears severe, uncompromising. When Jesus drove the money-changers out of the Temple,

the people were seeing the stern side of God's goodness. Remembering that goodness is the perpetual desire to do good to others to the utmost of our ability, how might goodness appear to others when we apply the truths of Prov. 20:30 or 2 Thess. 3:10?

Lloyd Ogilvie in *The Magnificent Vision* says that when he gets out of bed in the morning, he has what he calls a "goodness time." Aloud he quotes or sings scriptures about the goodness of the Lord. Then he lists recent evidences of the Lord's goodness in his life. After that, he reclaims this fruit of Christ's character as he sings the chorus *God is so good, / God is so good, / God is so good, / He's so good to me!* Then he prays for each one he'll meet that day and asks for the flow of God's goodness through him to be perfectly mingled with knowledge and the sensitivity to speak the truth in love.[4]

Ogilvie declares that his best days begin with this kind of quiet time and that his least effective days are those when he doesn't take time to open his heart to the inrush of the goodness of the Lord.

The fruit of the Spirit is goodness—pure goodness, generous and utterly without guile. Ask God to make this fruit evident in your life.

Memorize: "How great is your goodness, which you have stored up for those who fear you, which you bestow in the sight of men on those who take refuge in you" (Ps. 31:19).

Prayer: *Dear Lord, I celebrate Your abundant goodness. I want to be like You. Make me good, so that You can use me to help fulfill all Your desires to be good to those in my life. In Jesus' name I pray. Amen.*

8

FAITHFULNEſſ

FAITHFULNESS is always doing what's right when we feel like it as well as when we don't. If we're faithful, we do what we'll have wished we had done when we see things in eternity's light.

Portrait of Jesus' faithfulness. Paul specifically tells us to "Be . . . faithful in prayer" (Rom. 12:12). Jesus did that. He not only prayed all night before major decisions, but He prayed for individuals. "Simon, Simon, Satan has asked to sift you as wheat. But I have prayed for you, Simon, that your faith may not fail" (Luke 22:31-32). He had been praying for Simon Peter by name! Evidently this was one of His prayer habits. And He has not abandoned that habit. Even now He is seated at His Father's right hand interceding for us—and I believe He still prays for us by name.

His faithfulness in us. A few days before Christmas, a close friend with whom we exchange gifts called. "When could you come over for our Christmas celebration?" I asked, glancing at our calendar. Unfortunately, we discovered there were no mutually free nights.

Later she told me, "You know, it hurt to realize we hadn't made our time together a priority. However, God used that incident to show me that that's how He feels when 'lesser things' usurp my time with Him. Even though I say that knowing God is my priority, if I order my schedule around other pursuits, then He's not a priority. My actions identify my priorities."

We like to think our desires indicate our priorities, but actually a glance at our daily schedule and calendar gives a more accurate portrayal. Faithfulness to a friend—and to God—is not determined by what we desire to do or even by what we profess we do. Faithfulness is based on what we actually do. "Many a man claims to have unfailing love, but a faithful man who can find?" (Prov. 20:6).

It's easy to say as Peter did, "I'll never deny You, Lord!" Our actions, though, tell God what we really are.

This fruit of the Spirit is of great worth. Some day Jesus will say, "Well done, good and faithful servant! You have been faithful with a few things; I will put you in charge of many things. Come and share your master's happiness!" (Matt. 25:21). The effort we've exerted to be faithful will then seem as nothing.

Let's consider God's faithfulness to us and then look at areas in which He hopes to find us faithful.

Reflections on God's Faithfulness

1. When two words are frequently linked together in the Bible, it usually means they're nearly synonymous or at least have some special bond. What two words describing God are linked in Pss. 25:10; 36:5; 57:3, 10; 108:4?

2. What similarities or special bond do you see in these two words? How important are they to each other in a relationship?

"He is the faithful God, keeping his covenant of love to a thousand generations" (Deut. 7:9). The covenant He has made with us is not an agreement made years ago that He must keep simply because He gave His word. It's a covenant of love. Because He loves us so much, He's faithful always to give us as much as He can in response to our prayers and trust in Him.

3. Read the following verses, which speak of His faithfulness, and record the phrases that mean the most to you.

Exod. 34:6

Deut. 32:4

Ps. 91:4

4. Notice that in the following verses, the psalmist based his appeals on God's faithfulness.

Pss. 86:15-16; 115:1

5. The faithfulness of God is "His determined loyalty to a gracious covenant."[1] How confident is God that He will keep His covenant? See Jer. 33:20-21, 25.

God will never break the covenant, but He spoke of the possibility of our breaking a covenant He makes with us. He stated this plainly in Gen. 17:14: "Any uncircumcised male, who has not been circumcised in the flesh, will be cut off from his people; he has broken my covenant." (Circumcision was "a symbol for purity of heart and readiness to hear and obey.")[2]

God is seeking a love relationship with His people. No bridegroom wants a bride whose will he has to coerce—either to enter the relationship or to stay in it. He wants a *continued* love affair.

God desires that from us—a moment-by-moment intimacy. He says, "I will always be faithful and show you My love. All I ask of you is your continued love and faithfulness."

To believe that God makes a covenant with us that we cannot break is to destroy the beauty of our love relationship with God. The constancy of our relationship with Him is like that of a husband and wife who are joined together by a covenant. For the relationship to continue, both must be faithful.

We need have no fear, though. God promises grace to help us be faithful. We have to rely not upon ourselves, but upon Christ within us.

6. Paul is confident that God is able to keep us faithful even in temptation. What are God's promises in the following passages?

1 Cor. 10:13

2 Thess. 3:3

Reflecting His Faithfulness

Faithfulness, a fruit of the Spirit, is *His* fruit, not just a product of our own efforts; we receive it from Him as we rest in Him. We grieve the Spirit, though, if we don't do our part to be faithful. In this section we'll consider some of the areas Scripture speaks of regarding our need to be faithful.

1. *Am I faithful in friendship?* Constancy in adversity is a loyal friend's outstanding feature. Fair-weather friends are many. See Prov. 19:4, 6-7.

2. We're especially encouraged to be faithful to friends of our parents in Prov. 27:10. Why is this wise advice?

3. True friends, though, love at all times, according to Prov. 17:17. According to 11:13, what is one sign of a faithful friend?

4. Consider who you would call a faithful friend. Why do you consider him or her loyal?

5. *Am I faithful in serving God?* Faithfulness was Paul's basis for being chosen to be in God's service. See 1 Tim. 1:12.

6. In 2 Tim. 2:2 what kind of people did Paul instruct Timothy to train?

7. Why do you think God said the qualification for those in His service should be faithfulness?

If we're faithful, our lives can be scrutinized in even small details. We're true to our word and meet our appointments. Letters are answered, bills punctually paid. The interests of others are important to us.

8. See Titus 2:10. Why does faithfulness, or our lack of it, affect how attractive our doctrine is to others?

A missionary said that when he was young he asked an older missionary, "What's the one most important quality I should have?" The older man thought for a bit and then replied, "Always keep your word." Many years later he sees the wisdom of that statement. Why was this wise advice?

9. *Am I faithful in prayer?* One night a lady in Florida began to pray for her unsaved landlord. God helped her pray into the night. As she interceded, God began to encourage her faith. Suddenly the thought came to her, "But he's an alcoholic—he'll never get saved." She climbed back into bed and slept the rest of the night.

Weeks later, the landlord's wife told the praying lady an amazing story. "One night my husband was restless. He was feeling miserable and was unable to sleep. Finally, he got out of bed and headed toward the church across the field. But just as he got to the door and put his hand on the doorknob, his distress left him. He came back home, climbed into bed, and went to sleep."

"Be . . . faithful in prayer" (Rom. 12:12). What are some practical ways you can encourage yourself to apply Gal. 6:9 in prayer?

10. We show our faith in God by praying when we don't have any reason other than faith to believe that our prayers are effective. One of the key indicators of the strength of our faith is whether we continue to wait before God even when the answer is slow in coming. Write at least one insight you get from Luke 18:1-8 to encourage your faithfulness in prayer.

11. Have you been tempted to think, "I've tried to please the Lord, but I don't see answers to my prayers. Those who don't pray seem to get along just as well as I do. What good is there in making the effort?" In some of His final words in the Old Testament, God replied to this type of thinking. What does He say in Mal. 3:13-15?

12. If you don't see the faithfulness of God, be faithful anyway. One day He will show himself faithful. Read Mal. 3:17-18.

How Can I Grow in Faithfulness?

1. *Value the small opportunities to be faithful.* Notice that in Luke 16:10-11 we learn that a person's way of fulfilling a small task is the best way to know if he or she can be entrusted with a bigger task. This is true with all jobs, but Jesus may also be saying, "On earth you're in charge of things I've lent to you. I've made you a steward over them temporarily. In heaven you'll have what's really yours, and what I give you in heaven depends upon how you care for what I've given you on earth." What might be possible areas in which God will judge us for our faithfulness and reward us accordingly in heaven?

2. Opportunities to pay off big debts are rare, but we often have many chances a day to save a dollar. If all these chances are multiplied by 365, the total represents a respectable sum. I came across an old notebook in which my father had written down all the purchases he had made on a daily basis—even the five-cent ones. If you kept such a record, in which types of purchases do you think you might later wish you had been more selective?

3. Consider how David's habit to faithfully do what he could prepared him for the moment he stood before Goliath. (Read 1 Sam. 17:26-50.) David's first assignment was not Goliath, but to care for his father's sheep. Encounters with the lion and bear enabled him to see he could do anything needed with the Lord's help. What are other responses David could have given when confronted with a lion or bear?

4. God often wants to prepare us for greater tasks when he gives a small assignment. We are attacked and are prone to respond, "There's nothing I can do." David's determination to do all he was assigned to do prepared him to do greater works. Who would have thought that tending sheep would have shown his abilities? Our eagerness to seize daily opportunities is so telling. God sees either indifference and doubt, or faith that says, "God will help me do all I need to do." In what ways can you show God today that you're determined to be faithful?

5. *Have the right priorities.* Consider the priority the apostles gave to prayer. They learned that the widows were being neglected, and what could have been more important than caring for them? After all, "Religion that God our Father accepts as pure and faultless is this: to look after orphans and widows" (James 1:27). They somehow knew, though, that even caring for the widows was not to come before their praying. They found others to care for the widows and then said, we "will give our attention to prayer and the ministry of the word" (Acts 6:4). Are there adjustments you need to make in your schedule to make prayer a priority?

Sometimes people say they live to shop or someone says, "I live to eat." But if we're like Jesus, we live for a different purpose. What does Jesus live to do, according to Heb. 7:25?

6. In his book *Measure Your Life,*[3] Wesley Duewel discusses the importance of finding God's purposes in every area of our lives. Throughout the book he teaches that for each day we spend on earth, there will be billions and billions of future years in which we'll reap what we sow. Every second of every day will be of tremendous significance in eternity. Each moment we invest in prayer will pay eternal dividends.

What things do you have to do today? In eternity's light, which of these will have seemed important?

7. *Ask God.* A woman told me that one night she and her husband knelt to pray about her bleak job situation. "I led in prayer first, but I didn't pray long, because I was discouraged. Then my husband began to pray, and he prayed with a calm confidence that God is in control and that He is bringing good through all our troubles.

"Afterward I prayed, *Lord, give me the faith of my husband.*

"The next morning I awoke full of hope and fresh confidence in God." God has an abundance of ways to encourage us to be faithful. Sometimes we simply forget to ask. We try to rely on our own faithfulness rather than on His. Let's make it our habit to let Him know we're relying on Him to help us.

How good it is to know that we don't have to rescue

ourselves! A little lamb that has fallen onto its back can't roll over and get back onto its feet by itself. Our Good Shepherd knows that. He sees us as His little lambs and is ready to rescue us when we call to Him.

Memorize: "My eyes will be on the faithful in the land, that they may dwell with me; he whose walk is blameless will minister to me" (Ps. 101:6).

Prayer: *Dear Lord, thank You for being faithful to all Your promises and for protecting the way of Your faithful ones. Grant me the desire to have the priorities I will have wished I had when I stand before You. To the faithful You show yourself faithful. I rest in Your perfect provision, which provides all the strength I need to daily do all Your will. In Jesus' name I pray. Amen.*

(Scriptures used in this prayer include Ps. 145:13, Prov. 2:8, and Ps. 18:25.)

9

MEEKNESS
(GENTLENESS)

MEEKNESS* means accepting uncomplainingly what comes, trusting that a loving God orders—or at least allows with good purposes—all things. We're prepared to forego our rights in this world if that's what God requires.

Portrait of Jesus' meekness. Jesus laid His honors down and left heaven to live with creatures farther beneath Him than an earthworm is beneath a man. He made himself one of us and even called himself our Brother. He was always yielding to others, always holding back His power and not using it. He was continually subject to the will of people beneath Him until at last they nailed Him to the Cross. His whole life was spent carrying others' burdens and sharing their sorrows.

Loving sacrifice was Christ's self-imposed law. We're told, "Carry each other's burdens, and in this way you will fulfill the law of Christ" (Gal. 6:2).

His meekness in us. Dinner was over, and conversation had shifted to a philosophical tone. "Our society doesn't breed meekness," commented our dinner guest.

"How do you define meekness?" I asked.

His young daughter piped up, "Mouse!" Her response echoed the disdain most people have for this misunder-

---

*"Meekness" is used in the KJV, but in the NIV and other versions, it is often translated as either "gentleness" or "humility." Since the Greek word for "meekness" means both "gentleness" and "humility," both aspects will be discussed in this chapter.

stood fruit of the Spirit. To many, meekness often suggests weakness or effeminacy. It conjures up the cringing spirit of Charles Dickens's Uriah Heep, who said, "I am so very 'umble, Master Copperfield: so very 'umble."

Yet Christ used this fruit of the Spirit to describe himself. "I am meek and lowly in heart," He said in Matt. 11:29 (KJV).

Our dinner guest commented, "I see a lot of restraint in meekness. When an ordinary man tries to pick a fight with an eighth-degree black belt in karate who knows that with a flick of his wrist it would be all over, and he refuses to retaliate—that's meekness."

William Barclay would agree. He says that the most important quality of meekness is having oneself under control. The word in Greek is used to describe a tamed horse.[1]

The striking difference between the assertiveness the world says we're to exhibit and the meekness that imitates Christ is this: meekness does not assert itself for its own sake.

If we want to be Holy Spirit-filled Christians, we must act as the Holy Spirit acts. He always honored Jesus and showed humility by never speaking of himself. As His fruit enables us to act just as Jesus would, He reveals Christ to those around us.

The restraint of meekness frees us to maintain a gentle spirit as well as to benefit from criticism. I'll never forget the episode that taught me this aspect of meekness several years ago while I was working on an issue of *Women Alive*, the magazine I edit. I was reading in Deut. 5 the people's request to Moses: "Go near and listen to all that the LORD our God says. Then tell us whatever the LORD our God tells you" (v. 27).

Moses was a man qualified to speak to the people for God, and the people were willing to listen to him. I decided there must be a connection between Moses' ability to speak for the Lord and his being the meekest man on earth (Num. 12:3). I began to pray for meekness.

The next week I wrote an article and, as always, gave it to another to critique. She pointed to my main point and said, "I have serious problems with that paragraph." I wanted to ignore her comment, but it fell so close on the heels of my prayer for meekness that I was afraid to disregard her advice. Several days went by, and I continued not feeling clear before God to use the article.

I read the definition of meekness in *Nelson's Illustrated Bible Dictionary:* "An attitude of humility toward God and gentleness toward men, springing from a recognition that God is in control." Humility toward God and gentleness toward men! Had I been gentle? Maybe I hadn't been harsh; I had responded more with silence. But my response had been an unbending silence, not a *gentle* silence.

What a freeing concept! Because God was in control, I could afford to be humble before Him and gentle with others. God was going to be the One to decide about the article.

I went to the phone, called her, and confessed to her my wrong attitude. Would she forgive me?

"Yes, I forgive you, Aletha," she said.

Suddenly it didn't matter to me now if we used the article or not. All that mattered was that my attitude was pleasing to God. I had tried to do my part of being humble before God and gentle with her, so I knew God was in control. In the end, circumstances caused us to use the article, but using it at this point caused no hard feelings.

Reflections on Meekness

Meekness is possessing mastery over our emotions so we can respond with the mind of Christ—rather than out of selfish motives. As we master ourselves with the aid of the Holy Spirit, we'll be able to be servants of others.

According to John Wesley, there's no disposition more essential to Christianity than meekness. Yet this grace is probably the most caricatured and least valued of all.

1. Was Moses a weak, mousy sort of man? Remember what he did:
   - He slew the Egyptian because he felt compassion for the oppressed (Exod. 2:11-12).
   - He confronted Pharaoh, the absolute ruler of the land (5:1-3).
   - He led a million people through the desert (15:22).

What qualities would he have needed to do those things?

2. In Num. 12:1-3 we glimpse a family feud among Moses, Aaron, and Miriam. What are the most stressful situations in which people ordinarily find themselves? How would you rate job conflicts, family conflicts, and ego bashing? Do you see these in this passage? (Aaron and Miriam's slander implied that Moses was fond of power and was ambitious to usurp it.)

3. How is Moses described in Num. 12:3?

4. Memorize Nelson's definition of meekness: "An attitude of humility toward God and gentleness toward men, springing from a recognition that God is in control."

Remembering "God is in control" makes meekness possible in unpleasant situations. How does this definition describe Moses' attitude in this passage?

5. What indications do we have that God was in control? See Num. 12:4-15.

6. Moses stayed humble toward God by letting God defend if defense was needed. He also stayed gentle toward the people by refraining from lashing out at them in anger. He attempted neither to defend nor to vindicate himself. How are you prone to respond in stressful situations?

7. Note that Miriam seemed to know how far she could push Moses. Do you think people tend to try to take advantage of meek people?

8. In the end, the meek will have the last word. See Ps. 37:11 and Matt. 5:5.

An evangelist came to Alexander Whyte's hometown and in his preaching criticized the other ministers there. The next day, a man who heard the evangelist visited Dr. Whyte.

"I went to hear the evangelist last night, and he said that Dr. Hood Wilson is not a converted man."

Dr. Whyte, his face dark with indignation, jumped angrily from his chair. "The rascal! The rascal!" he said.

The visitor was amazed to see this godly man so furious, so he went on. "That wasn't all he said. He said you're not a converted man either!"

Dr. Whyte stopped dead still. All the fire went out of him. Sinking into his chair, he sat for a full minute with his face in his hands.

Then, looking up in sincere earnestness, he said, "Leave me, friend. I must examine my heart."[2]

To be meek means to honestly examine others' ideas while listening for whatever the Holy Spirit may be saying. If we close the door to others' ideas, we may close admittance to a truth God could give us no other way.

9. Meekness is more than being gentle with others in our outward actions—it's an inward conviction. In fact, Jesus taught that restraining our outward acts is not enough. Notice that in Matt. 5:21-22, Jesus ranks anger that goes no farther than the heart as murder. If we're angry at someone and yet manage to restrain ourselves from saying even one unkind word, we are in what kind of danger? See verse 22 and 1 John 3:15.

Reflecting His Meekness

Secular magazines don't call us to be gentle and humble. The natural person sees no good reason to cultivate this fruit of the Spirit. To those who are accustomed to doing their own will, meekness could easily appear as weakness or wimpiness. We're advised, "Defend your rights! Be assertive!"

1. How does God view meekness in women? See 1 Pet. 3:4. Why do you think God places such a high value on meekness?

2. Perhaps the most basic reason we should seek to be humble is that if we want to be in harmony with the Holy Spirit, we must have the gentle, humble spirit He has. If we want the Holy Spirit to abide with us, to be at home within our spirits, we must be of the same mind as Christ.

How does Matt. 11:28-29 tell us to find rest?

Think of yourself as yoked to Jesus, and when you're wondering, "What would Jesus do in this situation?" He says, "I would be kind and gentle." As we keep looking to Him, we find rest.

When Jesus says, "Learn from me, for I am gentle and humble in heart, and you will find rest" (v. 29), we know there's no rest apart from humility. Why does pride cause unrest?

3. The meek person gets the added benefit of being able to make good decisions. See Ps. 25:9. George Mueller said that before he could discern God's will in a matter, he had to have no will of his own, but feel as though he wouldn't turn his hand to change the outcome. As long as he knew God was in control, that was all that mattered. Why can the meek be easily guided in decision making?

4. If meekness is gentleness, humility, and a belief that God is in control, a lack of meekness is harshness, pride, and taking things into our own hands. How could each of these keep us from being guided by God?

5. A meek spirit is a good witness to others. Larry said that before he became a Christian, he would pick a fight just because he enjoyed a good fight. When another person would do something Larry didn't like, he would clench his fist and shake it at him. One day after he had given his heart to Christ, Larry's unconverted wife said, "You can't do that any more—you're a Christian." He thought, "She's right."

"And you know," he added, "I haven't even felt like doing that for several months now."

Notice that Eph. 4:1-2 indicates being meek (often translated "humble" in versions other than the KJV) will demonstrate to others the sincerity of our walk with the Lord. Why is meekness a reasonable expectation of those who live for God's glory?

6. Humility is simply honesty in God's presence. "One of the men in my group doesn't project his voice enough. He says he wants to have a spirit of humility and feels that he shows more humility by speaking quietly." Several of us were facilitators of small groups in a speaking seminar, and we had met for a training session. Our leader shook her head and said that humility is not necessarily shown by voice tone or volume. Humility is a spirit that is conveyed

through our attitude. What might be things people do that they think others will interpret as humility?

7. Others receive our reproofs more easily if we have a spirit of humility. See 2 Tim. 2:24-25. What opportunities do you have to apply this truth?

8. One result of this fruit is abundant peace. See Ps. 37:11. Inner peace can be described as not fretting about the fact that we deserve better than we're getting. For example, while waiting in the express line at the grocery store, you count the number of items in the basket of the person in front of you. If there are several items over the allowed number, would you be tempted to cast hostile looks at the other shopper or think impatient thoughts? Would it help to remember that God is in control of your time?

9. What areas of our lives will meekness affect, according to the following verses? Consider why humility and gentleness are essential in each.
2 Cor. 10:1

Gal. 6:1

1 Pet. 3:15

When the Holy Spirit indwells us, He will be able to mellow our dispositions so that we can forgive those who injure us and can be gentle toward them. It is the meek who follow most closely to Christ and who are the most useful in His service.

10. In what spirit did Paul appeal to the Corinthians? See 2 Cor. 10:1 again. How important is this spirit in leadership?

Memorize: "Take my yoke upon you and learn from me, for I am gentle and humble in heart, and you will find rest for your souls" (Matt. 11:29).

Prayer: *Dear Father, may the gentle and humble attitude that was in Christ be in me. As I look to You, I know I can safely trust You to guide me in every situation. Thank You for providing me grace to have the quiet spirit that You highly value. In Jesus' name I pray. Amen.*

10

ſELF-CONTROL

SELF-CONTROL is by faith placing ourselves under the Holy Spirit's control. When the Spirit controls us, we have freedom to be all God wants us to be.

Isa. 58:13 speaks of "not going your own way and not doing as you please or speaking idle words." After we've offered ourselves to be totally devoted to God, not doing our own pleasure is our reasonable service. Self-control is a refusal to give in to the desires that give us pleasure when those desires differ from our call to discipleship.

Portrait of Jesus' self-control. Jesus' "inner control" was a result of His desire to give God glory. "I seek not to please myself but him who sent me" (John 5:30). His hunger to glorify His Father led Him to pray, "Father, the time has come. Glorify your Son, that your Son may glorify you" (17:1), even though the answer to His prayer meant His death on the Cross. As we make the Spirit of Christ at home within us, that same desire to give God glory will motivate us to do all for His glory rather than to please ourselves.

His self-control in us. Pastor Sai Lequeti is part of a worldwide partnership between The JESUS Film Project and the Church of the Nazarene. Before his team began their work of showing the *JESUS* film in an area of much spiritual darkness, Pastor Sai spent 40 days fasting and praying.

In one village, Pastor Sai was asked to pray for an elderly man, a stroke victim whose left side had been paralyzed and board-stiff for nearly four years. Sai got onto his knees. Taking the man's hand, he prayed and then commanded, "In the name of Jesus, stand up!"

Troubled and afraid, the man stammered, "No . . . no . . . I can't."

"Yes, you can!"

"No . . . I can't move." Then, to the amazement of all, the man rose to his feet.

Again, Sai commanded him: "Now, in the name of Jesus, walk!"

"No . . . I can't do it."

"Yes, you can . . . you can!"

"But I can't move!"

Sai encouraged him over and over: "God has healed you. Now walk!" First he took one baby step, then another. Soon he was freely walking around the room glorifying God.[1]

This healing illustrates the cooperation required between us and the Holy Spirit to produce the fruit of the Spirit. Before Christ comes in, our appetites and passions control us. Just as the stroke victim could not move for four years, those without Christ are unable to control their desires. "Those controlled by the sinful nature cannot please God" (Rom. 8:8). They are like Peter the Great, who said, "Alas, I have civilized my own subjects; I have conquered other nations; yet have I not been able to civilize or to conquer myself."[2]

When the Holy Spirit comes, giving us a spirit of self-control (2 Tim. 1:7), we have a new freedom. "Be self-controlled," we're told. "Trust Christ within you to give you moment-by-moment strength to obey."

One of the last verses of the Old Testament speaks prophetically of the coming of Christ: "For you who revere my name, the sun of righteousness will rise with healing in its wings. And you will go out and leap like calves released from the stall" (Mal. 4:2).

The use of the word "sun" to refer to Christ is interesting. Our sun is the source of all the energy on planet earth. Likewise, Christ is the source of all the energy in our spiritual lives. When we have Christ, our hope of glory, living within, we have new hope. We're tempted to think like the stroke victim, "But I've never been able to exercise control in this area before."

Jesus replies, "Trust Me. Go in *My* strength. You have access to new strength now."

And, amazed, we walk as we've never been able to walk before.

Reflections on Self-Control

1. According to Rom. 8:5-9 and 2 Cor. 3:17, what are the differences between those controlled by the Spirit and those controlled by the flesh?

2. Explain why being Spirit-controlled gives us the freedom to be self-controlled.

3. "I'm running hard for the finish line. I'm giving it everything I've got. No sloppy living for me! I'm staying alert and in top condition" (1 Cor. 9:26-27, TM).

The *New Living Translation* says it like this: "I run straight to the goal with purpose in every step. I am not like a boxer who misses his punches. I discipline my body like an athlete, training it to do what it should. Otherwise, I fear that after preaching to others I myself might be disqualified."

Paul knew that to disregard self-discipline was to disqualify himself for the Christian race and that in the end he might lose the crown of life. What are some of the disciplines you as a Christian must trust Christ to help you demand of yourself?

4. The phrase "If it feels good, do it" has become a humanistic cliché we disdain. This moment's indulgence makes tomorrow's sacrifice more difficult. Yet, the opposite—a consistent self-denial—poses a continual challenge.

Someone said, "To desire ease is to embrace a deadly enemy." What are some of the deadly enemies ease invites?

5. When life is over, what will have seemed important? In what areas will you wish you had exercised more self-control?

6. The ultimate disadvantages of loss of control far outweigh the momentary satisfaction. Drinks are never worth the hangover; the illicit sexual encounter is never worth the ultimate consequences. If there is an area in which you would like to develop more control, write it down, and compare the immediate satisfaction with the ultimate result.

7. Lack of self-control hinders our testimony. A man was visiting a church, and the place was packed. One woman graciously offered him her seat, and the man was impressed. When it was time to go home, the parking lot was equally full. He heard someone behind him honking impatiently. He turned around and saw it was the same woman who had so graciously offered him her seat in the pew. Her good had been undone. Her behavior was inconsistent and meant nothing. Can you think of other situations in which inconsistency or lack of control gives a poor testimony?

Reflecting His Self-Control

"God did not give us a spirit of timidity, but a spirit of power, of love and of self-discipline" (2 Tim. 1:7). Since the Holy Spirit gives the spirit of self-control, what role does He play and what role do we play in exercising this fruit? To examine this, let's consider both the self-control and the dependence on God the Israelites needed as they lived in Canaan.

1. When the Israelites entered Canaan, their land of rest, they had clear instructions to rid themselves of the enemies already settled there. What are some of the verbs used in Num. 33:51-53 that describe the actions they were to take?

2. We, too, are promised this Canaan-land rest. "There remains therefore a rest for the people of God" (Heb. 4:9, NKJV). We enter this rest by abandoning our own efforts to make ourselves holy (see v. 10) and by trusting in the provision of Christ's sacrifice for us.

Once we enter our land of rest, we'll find that within us are attitudes that are of the old life, ways that dishonor Christ. Now we're to rid ourselves of every attitude that doesn't surrender to the Holy Spirit. We must destroy all those ways that dishonor our Lord. Can we? Could the Israelites? See Num. 33:53.

3. What are some of the attitudes God expects us to drive out and destroy? Consider Gal. 5:19-21.

4. The land of rest was a land of conquest. The Israelites were promised continual victory if they fought the battles necessary to rid themselves of their enemies. If they did not, what were they promised? See Num. 33:55.

If they failed to drive out their enemies, God said, "I will do to you what I plan to do to them" (v. 56). Christians who permit themselves to have wrong attitudes and rebellious ways receive the same natural consequences as non-Christians.

The Israelites discovered that it was impossible to drive out these enemies without supernatural help. See Deut. 1:42-44.

It's a combined effort. Both our self-control and His supernatural provision are essential.

5. God cleanses us so we can give Him our total devotion, but what responsibility does He give us? Consider such verses as Eph. 4:25; 5:3-4; Col. 3:5-9.

6. The Holy Spirit enables us to see areas in which we need to develop self-control. We often don't realize how many ways in which we're almost unconsciously conformed to the culture and ways of the world. See Rom. 12:2. The Holy Spirit will faithfully teach us the areas in which we need discipline. See John 14:26 and 16:13.

7. The Holy Spirit gives us the power to become self-controlled. He does not treat us like robots and make our decisions for us. Rather, as we choose to obey, He empowers us to do God's will. See Col. 1:10-11 and 2 Pet. 1:3.

8. "The LORD gives strength to his people" (Ps. 29:11). Can you recall a time in your life when the Holy Spirit enabled you to do what you had tried and failed to do on your own?

9. Our role is to flee temptation. Too often we just crawl away, hoping it will overtake us. The secret to success is to avoid situations in which we're vulnerable. Notice the Bible's repeated admonition to flee evil.

Gen. 39:11-15

1 Cor. 6:18; 10:14

2 Tim. 2:22

10. What situations do you allow yourself to be in that make self-control difficult?

11. We also are to have holy habits. "We learn to order our souls the same way we learn to do math problems or play baseball well—through practice," states William Bennett in *The Book of Virtues*. Practice, of course, is the hard part. He quotes Aristotle's statement: "Whatever we learn to do, we learn by actually doing it: men come to be builders, for instance, by building, and harp players, by playing the harp. In the same way, by . . . doing self-controlled acts, we come to be self-controlled."[3]

Aristotle also tells us, "We are the sum of our actions, and therefore our habits make all the difference."

When someone admitted to a wise man that he was a person of few habits, the wise man replied, "Then you must waste a lot of time." Why do habits save both energy and time? How is our self-control—or lack of control—reflected in our habits?

12. List three habits you would like to have.

13. When will you begin them? To whom will you be accountable?

Reflecting Self-Control in Our Words

1. Write three insights you find in James 1:26; 3:2-6, on the importance of controlling what we say.

2. Do you think it's possible to have this outward sign of control without controlling our inner life? See Luke 6:45.

3. Why are our words important, according to Matt. 12:36-37?

4. "Death and life are in the power of the tongue" (Prov. 18:21, KJV). Words have enormous power when they penetrate a person's spirit. God wants us to view our words as words of value, words that will make a difference to those who hear us. Do you have the same confidence in the power of your words as Job had? See Job 16:5. Notice a similar truth in Prov. 12:25.

5. Notice four reasons given in Proverbs why restraining our words is praiseworthy.
    10:19

    15:1

    18:13

    25:15

6. Let's consider what kinds of words we should guard against.
    Guard against gossip. Gossip is sharing private information with someone who is neither part of the problem nor part of the solution. What does Prov. 11:13 imply about the one who refuses to gossip?

Guard against inappropriate speech. What kinds of inappropriate speech are mentioned in Eph. 4:29 and 5:3-4?

Guard against unkind words. What kind of law did the lady in Prov. 31:26 make for herself?

7. Others' reaction to us might be indicative of the kind of words we've said. For instance, if our children are upset, could they be responding to our lack of self-control? See Prov. 15:1.

8. Match the following references with the insights from Proverbs.
   a. Prov. 15:28
   b. Prov. 17:28
   c. Prov. 27:14
   ___ The wise know when to give compliments.
   ___ He is considered a fool, not who has unwise thoughts, but who speaks them.
   ___ The wise person does not allow himself to speak without thinking.

9. We fail to speak right words when we don't depend on God to give us direction through the Holy Spirit. How did Jesus know what to say, according to John 8:28?

Memorize: "His divine power has given us everything we need for life and godliness through our knowledge of him who called us by his own glory and goodness" (2 Pet. 1:3).

Prayer: *Dear Lord, give me grace to please You in all my ways, to push myself beyond the comfort zone. Protect me from embracing ease, to remember that You denied yourself nothing so that I might live. In view of Your mercy, I offer my body as a living sacrifice. May I be holy and pleasing to You. In Jesus' name I pray. Amen.*

LEADERS' GUIDE

Suggestions for Leaders

BECOMING THE DWELLING of the Holy Spirit is a cooperative effort. God said, "I am the LORD, who makes you holy" (Exod. 31:13), and yet we read "Make every effort . . . to be holy" (Heb. 12:14). Paul announced, "You . . . have clothed yourselves with Christ" (Gal. 3:27), but also instructed, "Clothe yourselves with the Lord Jesus Christ" (Rom. 13:14). He wrote to the Ephesians, "You are light in the Lord. Live as children of light" (5:8). God will make us holy, but as Paul wrote to Timothy, we're to "train [ourselves] to be godly" (1 Tim. 4:7). God makes us holy, but we receive His holiness through faith and obedience.

"Let's make our entire lives fit and holy temples for the worship of God" (2 Cor. 7:1, TM). As we grow in godliness, our spirits become holy temples for the Spirit of God. His Spirit then indwells our spirits until He is literally living His life through us. As we go as carriers of His presence, it's no longer us but Christ who is interacting with our friends, living in our homes, going to the office.

The questions in this study are of two types. One type asks that you look up and record what the scripture says. This is not to be done merely as an exercise, but as a listener who wants to better understand. The Hebrew word for "manna" means "What is it?" because those words sound like what the Israelites said when they saw the manna on the ground. Before God's Word can become manna to us, we, too, must ask, "What is it?" "What is it to me?" "What does it mean for my life?" Then, when we're eager to know, God gives us understanding, and His Word becomes bread for our spirits.

The second type of question aims to help you make application of truth, to assist you in changing the material into the spiritual so Christ can be formed in your life. Participation should be optional for all questions, but especially those that require a personal response.

Be willing to share what the Holy Spirit teaches you. Samuel Logan Brengle, one of the great leaders of The Salvation Army, believed in sharing his own personal experience. "I look upon God's dealings with my soul, not as something to be hidden in my own heart for my personal comfort and guidance, but as a trust for the tempted and hungry-hearted who will hear and read me."[1] God will make you a channel of His blessings as you share His work in your life.

Additional Chapter Comments

Chapter 1

The Holy Spirit was given so that we would never be alone, so that we would always have the companionship of God, the very heart of God, as we travel life's road.

The indwelling Savior is as truly within us as He was with the disciples. But how much better it is to have Him *within* us than to have Him simply *with* us! Read John 16:7. Have the group discuss why having Christ within us is better.

To walk in the Spirit is to recognize that He is present and abiding in us. How often, though, after we've asked for His presence, we treat Him as if He were far off! It might be helpful for the class to share what has helped them to become sensitive to the Spirit dwelling within them throughout their day.

As we gain in the awareness of His presence and consider Him to be truly dwelling within us, we learn that we're indeed "in Christ." We're dwelling in the One who loves us, who constantly guides us. "In him we live and move and have our being" (Acts 17:28).

He wants us to experience His presence with a new and astonishing inwardness and intimacy. He shall "be in you," said Jesus (John 14:17, KJV). He shall "abide with you for ever" (14:16, KJV). He shall "guide you into all truth" (16:13, KJV).

Chapter 2

Jesus gave the command in John 13:34 that His disciples should love one another as He had loved them. Then in 15:9, He said He loved them as the Father loved Him. If we put these two verses together, we hear Him say that the love of God to Christ and the love of Christ to me and my love to others is one and the same love. What an immense thought!

We're tempted to say, "We can't love others as Christ has loved us." It *is* possible, though. The Holy Spirit pours His love into our hearts, and this love "knows no limit to its endurance, no end to its trust, no fading of its hope; it can outlast anything. Love never fails" (1 Cor. 13:7-8, PHILLIPS). The love the Holy Spirit gives takes the best and kindest views of all people and all situations as long as it's possible to do so.

Sometimes we pray for deliverance from an unloving situation when God is saying, "Trust Me to give you sufficient grace." Ask the group if there's a person or situation they want to see changed but through which God may be saying, "Trust Me to love that one through you."

Chapter 3

We realize that God commands us to love, but we often forget that He also commands us to be full of joy. "For the kingdom of God is . . . righteousness, peace and joy in the Holy Spirit" (Rom. 14:17). God wants us to live righteous lives and to have His peace, but it's equally important to Him that we have joy.

Jesus promised abundant life, but the lives of many Christians don't reflect His promised overflow of joy and peace. Many today are as stressed as their unbelieving friends. In fact, the psalmist said he, too, had almost despaired: "I had fainted, unless I had believed to see the goodness of the LORD in the land of the living" (Ps. 27:13, KJV).

In the next psalm the writer appears to have a fresh vision of God's ability to help His people: "The LORD is my strength and my shield; my heart trusts in him, and I am helped. My heart leaps for joy and I will give thanks to him in song" (28:7). How important is faith in maintaining joy?

Paul and Silas rejoiced because they were counted worthy to suffer for that name. We all have things that cause us to rejoice. What really gives you joy? Is it a joy in God? A joy in your own recognition? Is your joy in God's being glorified or in your own glory? Is it in meeting another's approval, or is it in the knowledge that you've done your best for Him?

If God's presence distinguishes us from the world, what kinds of things will give us joy? Have the group discuss how our joys will differ from that of the non-Christian as we learn to find our joy in pleasing the Lord.

Nothing reveals more accurately what we love than what gives us joy. If we love God with all our hearts, knowing He is pleased satisfies us completely.

Chapter 4

From ancient times, the hearts of people have longed for this peace—inner spiritual tranquillity. In the early days of Israel, the priests blessed the people by saying, "The LORD lift up his countenance upon thee, and give thee peace" (Num. 6:26, KJV). The Sanskrit invocations end with "Peace, peace, peace." The Muhammadan greeting is "Peace be upon thee." The answer to this longing is given in the words of Jesus: "Peace I leave with you, my peace I give unto you" (John 14:27, KJV), "that in me ye might have peace" (16:33, KJV).

One of the clearest evidences of the Holy Spirit's presence is a peaceful spirit when peace would not be a natural response. "Jehovah-Shalom" means "God is our peace" and was spoken to Gideon in a time of war in Judg. 6:11-24. Ask the class to consider why it's often in the midst of difficulties that God's peace is most evident. They may be willing to share times in which the peace of God was most evident in their lives.

Chapter 5

An impatient spirit is an unhappy spirit. It's a spoiler of happy conditions. Someone has said, "Impatience is a great weakness of faith." Why is this true?

It's important to keep inwardly holy. Impatience is subtle. It's natural to side with ourselves when the Holy Spirit reproves our impatient attitude. We think, *There was good reason for my conduct.*

In his book *Impatience and Its Remedy,* Milton L. Haney said that as a barefooted boy, when he would stub his toe against a root, he would pick up a club and beat the root. If he hurt his finger with a hammer, he would throw the hammer to the ground. This is the spirit of revenge. When this spirit rules us, we desire to do injury. He suggests that a scolding spirit is from a desire to hurt somebody.[2] Would you agree? Do you think the Holy Spirit is at home in a scolding spirit?

Ask God for a heart like His. "The goal of this command is love, which comes from a pure heart" (1 Tim. 1:5). When we trust Him to purify our hearts, He displaces the irritable spirit with His Spirit, which is not rude, impatient, or unkind. His Spirit of love never fails.

The remedy for impatience is to trust God for a completely holy heart and then to have a walk with God in which His Spirit rules. When we're about to respond with an unkind outburst and His Spirit says, "I wouldn't go there," we keep in step with the Spirit.

Chapter 6

The ancient writers defined kindness as the virtue of the person whose neighbor's good is as dear to the person as his or her own. Yet, E. E. Shelhamer wrote, "Many secretly seek themselves in their actions, but know it not."[3] Those who may appear to be kind may be seeking their own good rather than the good of others. Discuss what you think he meant. How can we tell if through our kindness we're seeking our own good or the good of others?

To many people the word "kindness" suggests weakness and sentimentality. In fact, what may masquerade as or be called kindness can cause great harm.

Firmness is not incompatible with kindness. Kindness and permissiveness are not synonymous. Kindness does not mean that we passively ignore wrong. See this illustrated in the character of God in Exod. 34:6-7 and Num. 14:18.

Have the group discuss when permissiveness might indicate a lack of loving-kindness.

Have you experienced kindness when you felt particularly unworthy? What's the typical response to undeserved kindness? A discussion on this topic may encourage those who are showing kindness but receiving no indication that it's appreciated.

Chapter 7

"For God caused Christ, who himself knew nothing of sin, actually to be sin for our sakes, so that in Christ we might be made good with the goodness of God" (2 Cor. 5:21, PHILLIPS). God paid such an enormous price for us to have this quality of His character!

Often people pray for love, joy, peace, patience, or kindness, but seldom do we hear the heartfelt cry "O God, I just want to be made good!" Yet it's this fruit of the Spirit and the next one (faithfulness) that qualified the servant to receive more responsibilities and to enter his master's joy.

"His master replied, 'Well done, good and faithful servant! You have been faithful with a few things; I will put you in charge of many things. Come and share your master's happiness!'" (Matt. 25:21).

In fact, in Ephesians Paul limited the fruit of the Spirit to three: "The fruit of the Spirit is in all goodness and righteousness and truth" (5:9, KJV).

Goodness is hard to define precisely, because "good" is used to mean so many things that it means nearly nothing. We may say, "She's a good woman," and mean that she frequently volunteers at church, she's morally upright, or we enjoy her pleasant personality.

To have this fruit of the Spirit includes being morally upright, but we may be ethical for many reasons—pride, approval of others, habit. If we possess the fruit of goodness, we'll be good, guileless, and generous. Even our generosity can be a source of pride. Let's learn to look to Him for His approval and to be content with His words "Well done."

Chapter 8

All of us have people in our lives whose spiritual welfare depends upon our faithful vigilance in prayer. For parents, no one can more easily arouse our sense of need to protect than our children. In a questionnaire in *Women Alive!* magazine, we asked "What is your biggest concern?" By far, the most frequent response was for the spiritual welfare of their children. That sense of wanting to provide spiritual protection for them is one of God's gifts to mothers.

The moment we determine to pray daily, though, Satan seeks to distract us. When we have time to pray, we no longer feel the same inclination and have to fight listlessness. The children seem to be getting along fine without additional prayer. We kneel to pray and wake up 15 minutes later and think we might as well forget trying. Satan suggests that this is the perfect time to do that cleaning we had postponed.

Hudson Taylor said that Satan will find something to do to keep us from praying even if it's adjusting a window shade. He also will tell us that our prayers aren't effective since we're not really believing. He doesn't want us to realize that the mere fact that we're praying expresses faith. In the New Testament, one Greek word can be translated either "faith" or "faithfulness." On those days I find it difficult to know I'm trusting, I like to think God says, "I see your faithfulness, and that tells Me that you believe I answer."

When we choose to skip prayer, perhaps Jesus would say, "If you, even you, had only known . . . what would bring you peace" (Luke 19:42). Someday the rewards of faithful praying will be evident, and we will be so glad we continued to pray even when we could see no results.

Jesus, in whom the Spirit rested without measure, was a Man of prayer. Is our view of prayer as high as His? He saw it as absolutely essential to what He needed to do.

Chapter 9

Meekness has been called the virtue that we need most of all, and perhaps the reason it's difficult is because it requires humility. Humility allows us to care only that we have our Father's approval. Jesus sought to say and do what His Father wanted. He never resisted the will of God. He was so intent upon pleasing His Father that He said, "I do not accept praise from men" (John 5:41). He did not mean that if someone said, "Jesus, You're so kind," He would reply, "Oh, no—don't say that." He meant that it mattered to him only what God thought about Him. He would believe only what He knew God would say about Him. He constantly looked to God—not to others.

After we've been used by God, the temptation is to be glad to accept praise from others. Notice in Matt. 14:22 that after the feeding of the 5,000, Jesus had the disciples immediately leave the scene of their success. It appears that He did not want the disciples to remain where they had helped Him with a miracle.

Their part in handing out the miraculous bread might have caused some to praise them, and the praise may have turned into a temptation to pride. We should never dwell too long upon either past successes or failures. They tend to cause either pride or discouragement.

You might discuss with the group why pride and meekness cannot coexist. What kinds of things can we do to help avoid temptations to be proud?

Chapter 10

Self-control in the Christian life results in a positive, Spirit-enabled, and disciplined life. It's what Paul calls "walking in the Spirit." (See Gal. 5:16.) We teach children that self-control is doing something even when we don't feel like it. It's sometimes defined as "instant obedience to the initial promptings of the Holy Spirit."

The psalmist wrote, "My heart is steadfast, O God" (108:1). We begin to abide in Him by an act of our will, which says, "I choose to trust God in this situation, to have the mind of Christ, to say His words, to look to Him for guidance." Then we obey no matter the cost. Eventually the habit becomes established. Not that it ever fails to be a choice, but the choice becomes more automatic.

Finally we see progress. We instinctively hold our tongues in situations when we normally would have spoken. We remember to look to Christ before impulsively reacting. As we continue moment by moment to trust Christ and to obey Him, walking in the Spirit becomes as natural as breathing.

Notes

Introduction

1. Dennis Kinlaw, *Preaching in the Spirit* (Nappanee, Ind.: Francis Asbury Press of Evangel Publishing House, 1985), 20.

Chapter 1

1. *His Victorious Indwelling: Daily Devotions for a Deeper Christian Life,* ed. Nick Harrison (Grand Rapids: Zondervan Publishing House, 1998), 302.

2. Quoted in William Barclay, *Matthew,* vol. 2 of *The Daily Study Bible Series* (Philadelphia: Westminster Press, 1975), 16.

3. Kinlaw, *Preaching in the Spirit,* 19.

4. Donald Grey Barnhouse, *The Day-by-Day Christian Life: Keswick's Authentic Voice,* ed. Herbert F. Stevenson (Grand Rapids: Zondervan Publishing House, 1959), 384.

5. *His Victorious Indwelling,* 289.

6. Barnhouse, *Day-by-Day Christian Life,* 386.

Chapter 2

1. Andrew Murray, *God's Best Secrets* (Grand Rapids: Zondervan Publishing House, 1979), March 31 devotional.

2. George Watson, *Soul Food* (Cincinnati: Revivalist Office, 1896), 114-16.

3. Wesley Duewel, *Mighty Prevailing Prayer* (Grand Rapids: Francis Asbury Press of Zondervan Publishing House, 1990), 120.

4. Jerry Bridges, *The Practice of Godliness* (Colorado Springs: NavPress Publishing Group, 1996), 202.

Chapter 3

1. Robert La Franco, "The Top 40," *Forbes,* September 23, 1996, 165.

2. Quoted in A. B. Simpson, *A Larger Christian Life* (Harrisburg, Pa.: Christian Publications, n.d.), 25

3. Hannah Whitall Smith, *Everyday Religion* (Salem, Ohio: Allegheny Publications, 1988), 72.

4. Oswald Chambers, *He Shall Glorify Me* (Grand Rapids: Discovery House Publishers, 1946), 239.

5. Ibid.

Chapter 4

1. Jim Morud, "Through the Valley," *Worldwide Challenge* 26, No. 4 (July-August 1999) (published by Campus Crusade for Christ, Orlando, Fla.), 22.

2. Cynthia Heald, *Becoming a Woman of Freedom* (Colorado Springs: NavPress, 1992), 65.

Chapter 5

1. W. E. Sangster, *Pure in Heart* (Salem, Ohio: Schmul Publishing Co., 1984), 128.

2. Jeanne Hendricks, *A Mother's Legacy* (Colorado Springs: NavPress, 1988), 110.

Chapter 6

1. Bob Benson and Michael W. Benson, *Disciplines for the Inner Life* (Nashville: Generoux/Nelson, 1989), 376.

2. Karen Burton Mains, *With My Whole Heart* (Portland, Oreg.: Multnomah Press, 1987), 70.

3. Stephen R. Covey, *The 7 Habits of Highly Effective People* (New York: Simon and Schuster, 1990), 30.

Chapter 7

1. *God's Treasury of Virtues* (Tulsa, Okla.: Honor Books, 1995), 256.

2. John Piper, *The Pleasures of God* (Portland, Oreg.: Multnomah Press, 1991), 191.

3. Sangster, *Pure in Heart,* 146.

4. Lloyd John Ogilvie, *The Magnificent Vision* (Ann Arbor, Mich.: Servant Publications, 1980), 122.

Chapter 8

1. *New International Standard Bible Encyclopedia,* ed. Geoffrey W. Bromiley (Grand Rapids: William B. Eerdmans Publishing Co., 1982), 2:273.

2. *Nelson's Illustrated Bible Dictionary,* ed. Herbert Lockyer Sr. (Nashville: Thomas Nelson Publishers, 1986), 236.

3. Wesley Duewel, *Measure Your Life* (Grand Rapids: Zondervan Publishing House, 1992).

Chapter 9

1. William Barclay, *The Letters to the Galatians and Ephesians,* in *The Daily Study Bible Series* (Philadelphia: Westminster Press, 1976), 52.

2. Sangster, *Pure in Heart,* 161-62.

Chapter 10

1. Adapted from a May 1999 letter by Paul Eshelman on behalf of Campus Crusade for Christ.

2. W. J. Armitage, *The Fruit of the Spirit* (London: Marshall Brothers, n.d.), 90.

3. *The Book of Virtues: A Treasury of Great Moral Stories*, ed. William J. Bennett (New York: Simon and Schuster, 1993), 22, 101.

Leaders' Guide

1. Clarence W. Hall, *Samuel Logan Brengle: Portrait of a Prophet* (Chicago: Salvation Army Supply and Purchasing Dept., 1933), 225.

2. Milton L. Haney, *Impatience and Its Remedy* (Chicago: Christian Witness Company, 1911), 41.

3. E. E. Shelhamer, *Helps to Holy Living* (Kansas City: Nazarene Publishing House, n.d.), 6.

CPSIA information can be obtained
at www.ICGtesting.com
Printed in the USA
FFOW05n1522270314

9 780834 117785